PAID

P9-DDS-241

AMERICAN CHILDHOODS

A Series Edited by James Marten

Children for the Union

Children for the Union

Children for the Union

Union

The War Spirit on the Northern Home Front

JAMES MARTEN

Ivan R. Dee

CHICAGO 2004

Library of Congress Cataloging-in-Publication Data:
Marten, James Alan.
    Children for the Union : the war spirit on the northern home front / James Marten.
        p. cm.
    Includes bibliographical references (p.) and index.
    ISBN 1-56663-563-2 (alk. paper)
        1. United States—History—Civil War, 1861–1865—Children. 2. Children and war—United States—History—19th century. I. Title.

E468.9.M37 2004
974'.03'083—dc22

                                                            2003064601

For Linda

Contents

Acknowledgments

IT IS WITH GREAT PLEASURE that I thank Ivan R. Dee for the chance to write this book and to edit the series in which it was published, and for his close editing of the manuscript. As I have tried to balance my research interests in both the Civil War era and in children's history over the last few years, it has been rewarding to revisit the issues and stories I first explored in 1998 in *The Children's Civil War*. This is not simply the "Northern" half of the earlier book; rather, relying in part on the kind words and suggestions of many reviewers—particularly Peter Bardaglio—I recast the evidence, placed the Civil War era more securely into its nineteenth-century contexts, and added material on underage soldiers and drummer boys.

A number of friends, colleagues, students, and acquaintances contributed to this book. They include Peter Bardaglio, Vi Boyer, Mary Ruth Collins, Mark Dunkelman, Brian Faltinson, Gary Gallagher, Julie Gores, Frank Keeler, Karen Kehoe, Liam O'Brien, Enaya Othman, T. Michael Parrish, George Rable, Patricia Richard, Joan M. Sommer, and Elliott West. Marquette University provided aid in the form of travel grants, research assistants, and summer stipends; some of the work was completed during semester-long sabbaticals in 1994 and 1999.

J. M.

Milwaukee, Wisconsin
February 2004

Children for the Union

Introduction: A Struggle Touching All Life

AS THE CIVIL WAR burst into flames and fanned across the United States, the country's children were inevitably drawn into the conflict:

In Boston, a little boy named Gerald named his paper soldiers after local officers, lined them up, and blew them over, simulating the gusts of bullets and canister that would mow down human soldiers on countless battlefields.

In Cincinnati, the future Boy Scout leader Dan Beard and his friends played army more intensely, scrounging up discarded guns and blasting away at clay forts and at each other.

In Michigan, Anna Howard's father and older brothers went off to war, leaving Anna, her mother, and her younger siblings to fend for themselves on their homestead in the woods—forty miles from the nearest train station.

In Yonkers, New York, a little girl named Jeannette wished with all her heart that she could be a drummer in her big brother's regiment. She practiced and practiced, but when she finally asked the colonel to take her along, he turned her down.

In Minnesota, a boy just in his teens went off to war as a drummer; over the next few years he marched a thousand miles, saw hundreds of men lying dead on a single battlefield, and nearly died from dysentery.

In Brooklyn, students at a black elementary school "adopted" a regiment composed of black soldiers, raising money to buy supplies and medicine for the regimental hospital.

Throughout the North, to the tune of "John Brown's Body" (more commonly recognized today as the "Battle Hymn of the Republic"), Yankee children sang "We'll Hang Jeff Davis to a Sour Apple Tree."

And in Wisconsin, the father of Hamlin Garland went off to fight against his wife's wishes; when he returned two years later, having survived Sherman's March and many battles and skirmishes, his two young sons did not recognize him.

This is the story of these and thousands of other children who lived in the North during the Civil War era. It shows how children were integrated into the war by forces beyond their control, as well as how they chose to integrate the war into their own lives. It examines children as members of a culture that became increasingly dominated by the war; as members of families who lived with the fear and hardships brought by the absence and deaths of fathers and brothers; as members of larger communities that had to deal with the political conflicts and economic ramifications of the war; and as Americans who found their lives to be increasingly militarized, shaping their play and encouraging some to join the army at very young ages. Finally, it is the story of a generation that carried its wartime experiences into adulthood, using them to shape decisions and assumptions throughout life.

This is also, it should be noted, a story that is unfortunately restricted almost entirely to white children. Although historians have focused extensively on the lives of enslaved and free African Americans in the slave states, far less research has been done on the experiences of free blacks in the North during the antebellum period, and virtually none has been done on the period covered by the war itself. Part of this is due to their relatively small numbers. Although perhaps a quarter of a million free blacks lived in the North in 1860, they were a tiny fraction of the population. Even in Northern cities with the greatest concentrations of African Americans, they were barely noticeable, comprising only 3.9 percent of the population of Philadelphia, 3.1 percent of Detroit, 2.3 percent of Cincinnati, 1.6 percent of Brooklyn, 1.5 percent of New York City, and 1.3 percent of Boston. In Providence, Rhode Island, their percentage of the population had actually declined during the generations leading to the Civil War, from 7.4 percent in 1790 to only 3.1 percent in 1865. Although a middle class of black professionals, contractors, barbers, and hoteliers was slowly growing, the overwhelming majority— 87 percent in New York alone—worked as manual laborers. Most states denied suffrage to African Americans, and most public schools were segregated. Despite the fact that since the 1830s black abolitionists in the North had held national conventions to agitate against slavery, and although Frederick Douglass was one of the most famous Americans in the 1840s and 1850s, the only context in which most Northerners considered African Americans at all was as slaves. In rural parts of New Jersey an extremely slow process of gradual emancipation left hundreds of black men and women in legal bondage as late as the 1850s. Simply put, African Americans— at least those living in the North—were barely noticed by most Northern whites, and, as somewhat transient, poorly educated, normally poverty-stricken, and always hard-pressed members of a nearly invisible population, few African Americans left behind written records. As a result, although the glimpses we get of black children in the North suggest at least some obvious similarities with white children, African-American youngsters cannot play a large role in the story of Northern children of war.[1]

Although the war may have dominated the thoughts and activities of Northern youngsters between 1861 and 1865, most managed to carry on "normal" lives too. A number of boys entered the army as

drummers or infantrymen, and many children were forced to replace absent fathers and brothers in fields or shops, but the daily existence of most Northern children remained the same. The rhythms
of their lives were marked by sunrises and sunsets, school bells and
church bells, the milking of cows and the washing of dishes. They
may have spent parts of their days picking lint or knitting socks for
the soldiers, anxiously reading newspapers for word of local regiments, and praying each night for loved ones off fighting the
Rebels, but they continued to be children too. As one Civil War
child recalled decades later, life went on, even in wartime: "People
married and were given in marriage, business throve, and we boys
kept right on with our tasks and sports. Our bodies and our minds
developed with the passing years," and wartime cares and political
differences were forgotten "when we met on the ball field, at the
swimming hole or at our homes."[2]

Readers of *Children for the Union* will certainly gain a sense of
what it was like to be a child or youth at mid-century—the pastimes, relationships, and assumptions central to young people in
any culture at any time are visible even during the worst of times.
Despite bombs falling on their cities and troops occupying their
homes, children play with improvised toys, bicker with siblings and
pout over imagined slights from friends, struggle to do schoolwork,
complain about household chores, and flirt with fellow teenagers.
This was as true for Northern children during the Civil War as it
was for children in Belgium in 1914 or London in 1940 or Tokyo in
1945 or Kosovo in 1999. Nevertheless, *Children for the Union* inevitably concentrates on the ways children became part of the war
and the ways the war forced itself into children's lives. As one
Northern woman who was a very young child during the conflict
remembered, the war "made itself felt from the words and looks of
those about us; there was some struggle going on in the world
which touched all life, brooded in faces, came out in phrases and

exclamations and pitiful sights." Children comprised more than a third of the population in 1860; they could not avoid the war and could not be avoided by those who would make war. Like their elders, they caught the "war spirit" that made their childhoods unlike any that came before or after.[3]

CHAPTER ONE

Childhood in Antebellum America

ACCORDING TO A BOY living in a small town in upstate New York, Civil War–era adolescence was "the period in our lives when fancy runs riot. The world was our oyster and all that was necessary was to open it and partake."[1] Clearly this boy relished—and as an old man no doubt recalled through rose-colored memories—the era in which he came of age. Part of his youth spanned the Civil War years, during which the war culture that pervaded children's lives embedded itself in the flourishing children's culture of the antebellum era. Northern children's lives would follow familiar paths during the war, but those paths would often carry young Yankees into new adventures, force them into new responsibilities, and challenge their lives and assumptions in sometimes alarming ways. Yet the activities and attitudes they shared and the concerns and capabilities they projected would always be based on prewar notions. The experiences of Northern children during the Civil War did not occur in a vacuum, and the patterns of their antebellum lives provide a necessary prologue.

Play and Playthings

For most upper- and many middle-class children, the mid-nineteenth century was a time of wonder. Increasing numbers of commercially produced toys and games were becoming available, and a score or more children's magazines were being published at any given time. Of course, class, geography, and even religion limited children's access to all but the simplest homemade toys and pastimes. Americans who grew up on farms or in small towns frequently remembered childhoods without much in the way of toys or organized play. John Quincy Adams, who became a Methodist minister, recalled a rural New York of the 1850s and 1860s where "recreation was little thought of . . . and vacations were almost unknown." He looked forward to the games, singing, and eating of the annual Sunday School picnic; ice skated and played with a homemade sled in the winter; and did a little hunting and trapping. He could remember his father taking him swimming only twice while growing up. Another New Yorker recalled of her prewar childhood that "children did not have so much in those days, we appreciated what we did get." Her favorite pastimes were creating paper dolls out of newsprint, ribbons, and colored scrap paper, fashioning dyes out of grape juice. Whenever she happened to get some carpenter's red and blue chalk, she felt "rich." At about the same time a Quaker boy in far-off Ohio contented himself with virtually no toys until his older cousin came back from town with nine marbles, which, in a telling mispronunciation, he called "marvels."[2]

Yet a boy growing up in New York City could enjoy far richer play experiences. The future historian John Bach McMaster was born in Brooklyn in 1852, just three years after Adams. Yet his urban setting and relatively well-off family created for him a childhood that, between school terms, was filled with fun and games. "Our playground was the street and a vacant lot," he recalled, where boys played baseball, tag and "prisoners' base." They scrambled onto roof tops to fly kites, snowballed passing sleighs, and ice-skated in Central Park. Their toys included tops and marbles; their pastimes included parties where the boys and girls "danced the Lancers and the Virginia Reel, played Forfeits, Pillow and Keeps, Clap-in-and-Clap-Out, and Going to Jerusalem, ate ice cream and cake." McMaster earned money by shoveling snow and recycling old newspapers, but as fast as he got it he spent it on dime novels.[3]

Boys in Dansville, a small but bustling New York town, rambled through the countryside, plundering blackberry patches and chestnut trees, scouting out new swimming holes, and exploring new—to them—places in the woods, "where," one reported, "we would solemnly declare 'the foot of white man had never trod before,'" and which they might choose to believe was a secret Indian burial ground. Yet in addition to these timeless activities of boys, they also took part in much more modern pastimes. They organized a baseball club called the Actives, which played teams from nearby towns. And they read everything they could lay their hands on, from classic authors like Thackeray, Scott, Cooper, and Fielding to children's writers like Jacob Abbott and Mayne Reid.[4]

In addition to sports, outdoor games, reading, and other pastimes, American children—at least those with relatively affluent parents—enjoyed playing with commercially produced toys and games, many of which were designed to encourage educational and religious development. The Parker Brothers' Mansion of Happiness (the first board game in the United States, it appeared in 1832) and the more famous Game of Life helped children practice important life strategies based on moral absolutes. Children played The Mansion of Happiness simply by spinning a needle. If a child landed on a "virtue"—Purity, Honesty, Temperance, Prudence, Truth, Charity, Industry—he or she could advance six more spaces. Landing on Cruelty, Prison, or Ruin forced the player to start over, while becoming a Drunkard caused the player to tumble backward twenty-five spaces. The moral lessons were obvious. Other toys were marketed as purely educational. Child-sized trains and telescopes offered mechanical and scientific information. Despite their label as "Sunday toys," Noah's arks taught children about exotic animals from foreign lands. Walter Brooks remembered fondly the ark—the "requisite of every well-organized nursery"—that he played with on rainy days, when he paraded the pairs of animals in and out of the vessel's side door endlessly, noticing but not caring that the figures of Noah's family towered over even the largest animals and that the lion and the mouse were about the same size.[5] Puzzles made from maps of the United States taught geography, blocks taught rudimentary geometric principles, and the age-old game of Authors introduced youngsters to famous literary personalities.

The most popular nineteenth-century toys among children and adults alike were imitative: they helped children recognize the skills and values they would need as adults. One of the great growth industries of the time—at least in terms of toys—was the manufacture of dolls, which were the most ubiquitous examples of toys as educational tools. Lydia Maria Child, the author and abolitionist, argued that dolls could fill a wide range of roles in their owners' lives. "When little girls are alone," she wrote in 1831, "dolls may serve for company. They can be scolded, and advised, and kissed, and taught to read, and sung to sleep—and anything else the fancy of the owner may devise." Girls could also practice sewing and needlework by making clothes and other accessories.

"Dolls were supposed to be the beginning and the end of a little girl's amusement," wrote one woman who grew up at mid-century. She personally recalled owning three dolls as a child: "a joint doll—a wretched little manikin of a thing, always lacking an arm or a leg"; a shawl tied up in her nurse's apron; and her "best doll," with a cloth body and china head. The shawl doll was her favorite—it was more or less the size of a real baby—but she admired the deep blue eyes of the china doll. Unfortunately, like so many of the toys owned by this rough and tumble, self-described "tomboy," the china doll was soon broken, "the top of her china head scalped as by a tomahawk, and the sawdust oozing from her cloth sides."[6]

Of course, as Child suggested, imagination was still required to make these commercially produced toys come alive. Alice and Mary Kingsbury would arrange their many dolls into a congregation on the nursery floor, where they would respectfully listen as their slightly older brother Willie, wearing one of their mother's nightgowns, would preach a "long eloquent sermon." The writer Eleanor Hallowell Abbott recalled that she "had the usual number of dolls," but despite the fact that "they were often pretty, invariably amiable, and unmistakably pleasant to take to bed with one on a lonely night," they seemed to have left her cold. She did, however, express "a consuming passion" for paper dolls, "not the prim and prissy paper dolls of ordinary paper-doll commerce" but "freelance paper dolls . . . filched at random from old magazines or current fashion plates." Safely ensconced in the well of her father's huge desk, she would enact fairy tales and adventures and domestic melodramas. Eleanor cast her plays from the multitude of reading and advertising material that flowed into her well-to-do clergyman father's home in Cambridge, Massachusetts: the queen of England came from a Christmas magazine while "half-naked savages" were found in missionary pamphlets. Props—"stove, and bookcases and ploughshares"—came from mail-order catalogs, while a quintet of pet dogs were torn from *Kennel Magazine* and a whole stable of purebred horses galloped from the pages of a Midwestern horse dealer's catalog. In Eleanor's case, old-fashioned imagination combined with the worldliness that affluence and commercialism could bring to the luckiest children to create an active fantasy world. Such was certainly the case with Maggie Deland, who constructed "hollyhock ladies" out of flowers, feathers, blades of grass, and straw, and, taking her cue from Fox's *Book of Martyrs*, burned them at the stake![7]

After Fort Sumter, dolls would find themselves cast as soldiers and soldiers' wives in their owners' fantasies, including a Civil War–era equivalent to the 1970s' GI Joe. Uniformed in the colorful red, white, and blue uniform fashioned after the French Foreign Legion, complete with baggy red pants and impractical fez, the Zouave doll was enjoyed by many boys around the country, including two residents of the White House, Tad and Willie Lincoln.

One rather inevitable bit of foreshadowing appeared in the antebellum years when boys participated in that age-old pastime of testosterone-filled youngsters: playing army. As they would during the war, antebellum Northern children organized their own mock militia companies, drilling and holding faux battles. The practice was common enough that portrait artists frequently posed boys with military props like swords and drums. But this activity was not described in prescriptive or religious literature as the sort of value-building, patriotic, and acceptable exercise it would become during the war. Civil War children would avidly apply their newfound knowledge of military and political affairs to prewar pastimes and toys, and would eagerly consume the war-related toys that borrowed from antebellum styles and mores.

Children's Literature

Children's magazines and novels were a vital source of war information and images for Northern children, and, as before the war, they were important complements to children's toys and games. The centrality of reading in the lives of many nineteenth-century children is revealed in numerous autobiographies—although in some cases authors may well have exaggerated their studiousness for the benefit of what many believed to be much more frivolous modern generations. In the 1860s every "real he-boy" in Cincinnati "signed his name in blood on the flyleaf of his favorite books." A boy growing up on the frontier cherished every book he ever owned or even touched. His Quaker father boasted a "library"—two shelves filled with Quaker tracts, the writings of William Penn, John Woolman, and George Fox—and the little boy loved the dog-eared copies of a Webster speller, Pike's arithmetic, Emerson's primer, and McGuffey's *First Reader*. The first book he ever owned, which he obtained by trading his only toy to a friend, was a copy of *Parley's Geography*. To him, the pictures and maps made it "a treasure of great value." A little later he received a copy of Charles Dickens's *Child's History of England*, which he absorbed sitting in a secluded spot behind the house. When his father returned from market one day, he received an unusually generous surprise: *The Surprising Adventures of Robinson Crusoe* (which the old Quaker assured his wife was a fine book, "very instructive and truthful").[8]

In educating American children, though, not books but children's periodicals did the heavy lifting—at least among the middle-class, mostly Northern children whose parents could afford to subscribe to them. A suggestion of the popularity of the many children's magazines published during the antebellum period appeared in an 1829 story in the *Juvenile Miscellany*, in which a family of children race for the door when the mailman delivers the latest number of the *Miscellany*. They nearly tear the magazine apart in their enthusiasm, but among the sections attuned to various ages, everyone gets a chance to look at his or her favorite. Many years later a real-life reader reported a similar scene. On the day the *Miscellany* was due for delivery, remembered one subscriber, "the children sat on the stone steps of their house doors all the way up and down Chestnut street in Boston," and as the mail carrier zigzagged his way down the street, he left delighted groups of little ones poring over the new issue.[9]

The first periodical for children published in the United States, *The Children's Magazine: Calculated for the Use of Families and Schools*, had lasted only four months in the 1790s. Yet it set the tone for dozens of children's magazines to come with its cautionary tales, religious content, and educational features, such as articles on world geography. Other early periodicals for children—normally for juveniles but sometimes for younger readers too—included the short-lived *The Fly; Or Juvenile Miscellany*, somewhat atypical for its inclusion of Boston theater reviews; *The Juvenile Port-Folio and Literary Miscellany*, begun in 1812 by a fourteen-year-old Philadelphian as concerned as older editors with high moral and intellectual standards; and *The Family Pioneer and Juvenile Key*, published by a Maine printer and his sons for several years after 1819, which offered didactic literature but also lurid crime and disaster stories from around the world. Between 1802 and the Civil War, at least 75 new children's magazines were begun in the United States; from 1840 to 1870 the number soared to more than 130.[10]

Two notable early magazines for children included Louisa May Alcott's *Juvenile Miscellany* and Nathaniel Willis's *Youth's Companion*, which began publication within months of each other, in 1826 and 1827, respectively. Willis's magazine was dedicated to pious letters telling of dramatic conversions and stories with titles like "Death Bed Scene of a Child Six Years Old" and "A Child's Prayer for His Minister." Virtually without illustrations and devoid of any kind of games or riddles, the *Companion* promoted a Calvinist version of middle-class values. Although modern readers would find the *Miscellany* stiflingly didactic, it was virtually freewheeling compared to the stiff religiosity of the *Youth's Companion*. It too sought to nudge readers into a pious, middle-class respectability, but with a wider range of stories and articles and from a liberal Unitarian philosophy. Its sermons, dialogues, biographies, and fiction, as well as its conundrums and poems, were seasoned with calls for children to work hard, mind their parents, live frugally, persevere in hard times, and trust in God. The columns of the monthly *Miscellany* were filled with poor children rising in the world—not to great riches, necessarily, but to respectability and comfort appropriate to their ambition, virtue, and class—by following the tenets of middle-class values.

A number of religious denominations published their own periodicals for children. The American Sunday School Union produced *Infant's Magazine* for, as its title suggests, the youngest children, and *The Child's Friend* for older readers; the *Youth's Instructor*, published by the Seventh Day Adventist Church, began its long run into the twentieth century in 1852; the Episcopalians put out *Children's Magazine* for two generations in the middle of the century; Mormons offered their children *The Juvenile Instructor*, and Presbyterian children could read *Forward*. The latter two magazines, each published under several different titles, continued for generations. All provided conservative, didactic reading material, Bible studies, denominational news, and other religious material.[11]

These magazines, writes the historian Ann Scott MacLeod, provided "a record of what adults wanted of and for the next generation," and they shared the assumptions and values of a wide range of American religious, educational, and political institutions. Secular as well as denominational magazines had long undergirded the moral and social assumptions of common childrearing practices. They promoted the principles of hard work, obedience, generosity, humility, and piety; trumpeted the benefits of family cohesion; and furnished mild adventure stories, innocent entertainment, and instruction. Authors of stories and novels as well as schoolbooks for children stressed character, framed the world in moral terms, and exuded confidence in the American way of life.[12]

Magazine editors encouraged their readers to embrace these values with features that sought to create a cozy community of readers with cheerful tones, kindly advice, and opportunities to correspond with writers, editors, and other readers. Oliver Optic wrote didactic editorials for the *Student and Schoolmate* from "The Teacher's Desk." *Forrester's Playmate* shared a monthly "Chat with Readers and Correspondence," and *Our Young Folks* (which first appeared in 1865) gathered children "Round the Evening Lamp." The format of these community-building sections varied from publication to publication. Some included games or brief notices of new children's books, and the more religious-oriented magazines like *Youth's Companion* filled their columns with inspiring obituaries (as late as the Civil War, *The Little Pilgrim* still featured the occasional saintly death of a treasured reader). Most editors responded directly to readers' queries, commented on the solutions to puzzles sent in by children, and sometimes—notably in *The Little Pilgrim*—encouraged readers to submit their own writing.

But one part of the world that they generally ignored was race. The relentless moralizing in children's literature between 1820 and 1860 tended to ignore politics and to focus on individual self-improvement. Publications for black children were virtually nonexistent. The *Christian Recorder*, an organ of the African Methodist Episcopal Church, included a section for children called "Our Children" or "Child's Cabinet," but even those poems and stories concerned themselves more with the development of moral values and obtaining salvation than with race.

Occasionally in the 1830s and 1840s a reference to slavery would appear in writing for children. In 1847, for instance, *The Anti-Slavery Alphabet* was published and sold to make money for the Anti-Slavery Fair in Philadelphia. Its preface told "our little readers" that despite their age there were many ways they could contribute to the anti-slavery cause.

> Even you can plead with men
> That they buy not slaves again . . .
> Sometimes, when from school you walk,
> You can with your playmates talk,
> Tell them of the slave child's fate,
> Motherless and desolate.[13]

Although short-lived periodicals like the *Slave's Friend* and *The Youth's Emancipator* urged children to form their own anti-slavery societies, the great national debate of the 1850s over slavery rarely

A is an Abolitionist—
  A man who wants to free
The wretched slave—and give to all
  An equal liberty.

B is a Brother with a skin
  Of somewhat darker hue,
But in our Heavenly Father's sight,
  He is as dear as you.

C is the Cotton-field, to which
  This injured brother's driven,
When, as the white man's *slave*, he toils
  From early morn till even.

D is the Driver, cold and stern,
  Who follows, whip in hand,
To punish those who dare to rest,
  Or disobey command.

A rare invocation of abolitionist sentiments in antebellum children's literature, *The Anti-Slavery Alphabet* was published for the Philadelphia Anti-Slavery Fair. *(Philadelphia: Merrihew & Thompson, 1847)*

appeared in juvenile books, textbooks, or even publications distributed by the American Sunday School Union—publishers feared alienating their potential customers.[14] Alcott's *Juvenile Miscellany* flourished for several years until in 1830 she began printing editorials and stories promoting racial equality and the abolition of slavery; subscriptions and sponsorships dwindled, and in 1834 she was forced to cease publication. A few children's writers expressed deep sympathy for the plight of the enslaved—though few acknowledged the existence of black people outside the institution of slavery—but their descriptions of African Americans rarely rose above vapid stereotypes. Even children's literature that was expressly abolitionist in outlook painted blacks as submissive and none too bright; they were nearly always caricatured victims rather than flesh-and-blood people. *The Anti-Slavery Alphabet*, for instance, concentrated almost exclusively on the hardships faced by slaves—featuring cruel drivers, bloodhounds, kidnappers, jails, the lash, slave auctions, and families torn apart—and provided simplistic Africans "rambling free . . . Delighting 'neath the palm trees' shade." Most abolitionist writers for children engaged slavery at the moral and political levels rather than at the human level, assailing what they believed to be the tiny minority of slave owners who were threatening to destroy the greatest government in the world over the immoral exploitation of their cruelly oppressed chattel. Others were more concerned with white abolitionist activists and "martyrs" like Elijah Lovejoy, killed by a pro-slavery mob in Alton, Illinois, in 1837. The limitations of these authors' racial vision were demonstrated when some accepted gradual emancipation and others, following Harriet Beecher Stowe's suggestion at the end of *Uncle Tom's Cabin*—considered by many contemporaries to be a book for children—agreed that everyone would be happier if the slaves were emancipated and then colonized to Africa.[15]

This changed during the Civil War, when virtually all children's magazines became thoroughly abolitionist and projected deep sympathy for the plight of African Americans. Furthermore, even as children's magazines and literature continued to stress antebellum values and priorities, authors for children began to edge away from excessive moralism and toward a more exciting and less didactic form of writing. High principles, family values, and a generic religiosity never disappeared from writing for children—especially in children's magazines—but they were diluted by the appearance of a much more exciting brand of children's reading material: escapist adventures and war stories. The Civil War played an important role in this transition, as popular magazines tended to place tried-and-true formulas in war contexts while juvenile novels began to explore the antics and exploits of their young heroes and heroines with less—or at least more superficial—concern for underlying moral truths.

Public Amusements

Like editors of children's magazines, proprietors of museums, panoramas, and other public amusements touted their attractions as morally and educationally sound. In the history and natural history museums of the early nineteenth century, biblical scenes were popular, of course, but entrepreneurs also offered fireworks, scientific experiments, and displays of microscopes and other technological innovations. Peale's Museum in Baltimore was established in 1813 to show off a mastodon skeleton. Other presentations included wax figures and historical paintings with patriotic and religious themes, and gymnasts, magicians, and ventriloquists displaying their God-given physical skills. Children, recruited with half-price tickets and special matinee showings, comprised an important percentage of museum audiences. To make their parents happy, entrepreneurs would bill almost any display as "educational."[16]

The actor Otis Skinner recalled Saturday afternoons as a small boy crossing the Charles River from Cambridge into Boston to wander the Boston Museum with his older brother Charlie. "A visit there was most instructive," wrote Skinner late in life, tongue firmly in cheek. The Hall of Curiosities held rows of shelves of minerals, stuffed birds, fossil remains, and busts and portraits of respectable, well-known gentlemen. It also contained an amazing display called Barnum's Japanese Mermaid, a "mummy, the size of a small cat, with female head, hair and breast, arms and claws of an animal and the tail of a fish." Although Skinner as a boy was "duly impressed" by this "ingenious piece of faking," he did "wonder why the Japanese were so clever in catching mermaids." One floor up was the true "place of dread," where Skinner "drank horrors by the bucketful": the waxworks gallery. Here were displays of Siamese twins; Daniel Lambert, "the celebrated fat man"; the Pirates' Cabin—complete with "corpses oozing blood, and pirates, armed to the teeth, gloating over them"; and the moralistic exhibition "Three Scenes in a Drunkard's Life." This last showed the downward spiral of a middle-class family. In the first scene they happily—and seemingly innocently—sipped champagne. The second portrayed them in a shabby house, down at the heels and succumbing now to rum; the third showed them at rock bottom: "daughter . . . had found profitable employment in the streets and had blossomed into colors like the butterfly." The father, "shrunken and haggard, a sore in the corner of his mouth, had just dealt Mother a blow with the gin bottle, and the poor soul lay prone in her dingy calico dress, rivers of blood ebbing from a hole in her waxen head. Son had become a moron, and Father was being arrested by a policeman at the very moment of murder." That the displays, ostensibly created as moral lessons, had an impact was confirmed in Skinner's frequent childhood nightmares and his frightening walks at dusk to a nearby bakery, where he was sure he would meet his end "in the dark corners that pirates and drunkards know about."[17]

Barnum's museum in New York City was one of the most famous museums of its time. Edward Mitchell, who moved with his family to New York as a boy, wrote many years later that "I thank and bless across the years the proprietor of the Fount of Eternal Youth"—Barnum—who would come out of his office behind the ticket booth on occasion and shake hands with young visitors. Mitchell "knew the Museum by heart," from many happy visits to the wax figure gallery, "the white whale in the basement tank," the row of Bohemian glass blowers, the demonstrations by the Lightning Calculator, and visits by "Grizzly Adams," with the silver plate in his skull and his trained bears. The lecture room offered "moral" entertainment—plays on reform or religious-minded topics like

"Joseph and His Brethren," "The Drunkard," and "Moses." Barnum himself would appear between acts, "stalk[ing] majestically before the advertising drop-curtain, leading his procession of dwarfs, giants, and living skeletons, and impart[ing] to the audience ideas of an ethical propriety to which no bigot could object."[18]

One popular form of public entertainment that would later be extremely valuable in presenting the war to home-front Northerners was the panorama. Originating in Europe late in the eighteenth century, panoramas had crossed the Atlantic early in the nineteenth century and were popular among city dwellers for their fantastic representations of scenery—the Mississippi River, mountain vistas, and the Holy Land were favorite subjects of panorama producers. The basic technology was quite simple: giant canvases—advertisements proudly proclaimed the thousands of square feet of surface occupied by the paintings—reeled across a wide stage from one large spool to another. A spoken narration and special music normally heightened the pleasure of the observers. One American panorama, which toured in 1815, showed people working at a number of occupations. It included a number of moving parts and the wax figure of a well-known, respectful slave woman who had worked at the Baltimore market for many years. A Boston boy recalled the "aesthetic contentment produced by no other spectacle, not even by the circus" when he attended showings of panoramas of "The Life of Christ"; Banvard's famous travelogue down the Mississippi River; polar expeditions; and his favorite, a tour of New York City, with its bustling streets, inspiring churches and hotels, and famous landmarks.[19]

All these forms of entertainment—like children's literature—had begun to evolve from at least ostensibly morally respectable programs to pure entertainment. Touring freak shows included animals with extra heads or limbs as well as people with astonishing deformities: bearded ladies and giants; Tom Thumb and other midgets; Chinese women whose feet, painfully bound when they were infants, had barely grown since. County agricultural fairs added spectacular activities like balloon ascensions, jousting tournaments, and their own distracting displays of the weird and unfortunate. The secularization of leisure was well under way by the time the Civil War broke out, and most of the genres of public entertainment adapted themselves to the events and meanings of the war.[20]

Community

The fact that children made up a third of the population in 1860 meant that they were literally everywhere, including at community events that in modern America are typically reserved for adults. Antebellum children frequently participated in the political meetings that provided election-year entertainment for the whole family. Indeed, a Pennsylvania boy believed that the parades and spectacles held by all the political parties "were . . . got up merely for our fun." He and his friends, he believed, were "in good part educated in American political life" when they attended every political debate and parade they could during the turbulent 1850s. When he was a little boy, James Sullivan recalled, another boy—obviously a Democrat—had whispered that a neighbor was "a Nabbo-Lisha-Ness" and that "he wants to marry his daughter to a nigger!" This common bit of racist propaganda certainly impressed James, who thought the old man "must be crazy." As he grew up, James became involved in politics in more sophisticated ways. The "hot politics" of the election of 1856 "broke me in to party parading, banner raising, badge wearing, and boys' electioneering by fisticuffs." The embarrassment of riches furnished by the four-way campaign of 1860 led James to attend every meeting and speech he could.[21]

The father of an Illinois teenager, knowing of his son's keen interest in politics, consented to take him to the Lincoln-Douglas debate in Charleston in 1858. The boy remembered the sights and sounds of it clearly nearly seventy years later. As the candidates mounted the debating platform, Harvey Magee recalled thinking that Lincoln "could easily pick apples from the top limbs of any of our apple trees without a ladder" and that the large-girthed Douglas would be hard to pin in a wrestling match. The boy was caught up in the excitement of the murmuring crowd and the banners carried by political "marching clubs" (including a "vulgar" cartoon of Lincoln with an arm around a black woman's shoulders above the caption "Negro Equality"). The speeches were not nearly as memorable as the atmosphere, but as an old man Magee held no memory "so precious as the one great privilege given to me of seeing and hearing Abraham Lincoln, the great Emancipator of four million slaves."[22]

The sectional crisis and the election of 1860 were among the first political memories of most Civil War children in the North. As one woman recalled of her circle of friends, "You can realize how strong feeling ran when eleven-year-olds wanted to go to a political meeting." At an event held during the election, she and her friends claimed seats across the middle of the front row, and "if anything was said against Abe Lincoln we would hiss." Apparently the adults in the crowd allowed the heckling to go on, for the speaker became flustered. At one point he looked down at the girls and said, "The hissing of geese once saved Rome, but the hissing of these East Hampton geese will never elect Abraham Lincoln president."[23]

Building on his initial exposure to politics, in 1860 Harvey Magee—still too young to vote—nevertheless joined the Republican "Wide-Awakes," who donned black caps and capes (partly, he recalled, to protect their clothing from oil dripping from the lamps they carried on poles above their heads) to campaign on behalf of Lincoln in the presidential election. They would appear at huge political rallies. At one of them, thirty thousand people crowded into a county fairgrounds to witness the uniformed marching clubs, decorated wagons and carriages (including a parade of wagons on which men were splitting rails in honor of Lincoln's nickname), and flags and banners. Ten cattle were slaughtered and barbecued for the occasion, and although the crowd was disappointed that Lincoln himself could not attend, Magee remembered it as an event "of great and memorable interest. I felt the spirit of liberty and patriotic enthusiasm which thousands of citizens had for Mr. Lincoln, and the cause of freedom."[24]

Henry Cabot Lodge was also struck by the appearance of the "Wide-Awake Clubs" on Boston Common, which became "a sea of tossing lights," more impressive than the banners and transparencies and fireworks and cheers of the other political parties. As a boy he "thoroughly enjoyed" the tumultuous political campaigns. As a United States senator many years later, he came to believe "that no more idiotic way of carrying on a political campaign was ever devised." More important was the stress of the secession winter. Although only nine years old, Lodge shared "my father's anxiety" and felt his own "sorrow and anger" after the surrender of Fort Sumter. Those emotions dominated his memories a lifetime later.[25]

A chilling precursor to war appeared in 1858 in the form of a comet—apparently the Comet Donati—which unnerved at least a few people young among Daniel Beard's family and friends. "The medieval prayer of 'Lord save us from the Devil, the Turk and the Comet,'" he recalled, "still lingered in their minds. In those benighted days comets were unmistakable signs of war." He knew some people claimed to have heard "the tramping of hundreds of feet at night" and "thousands of horsemen riding past"; newspapers reported "the appearance of towering clouds in the shape of the palmetto tree"—the symbol of South Carolina. His family tried to laugh off such superstitions, but "everyone was conscious of the ominous rumblings in the political world which made the startling and unannounced appearance of a comet quite disturbing."[26]

This no doubt impressed the ten-year-old from Cincinnati, and lent a greater urgency and interest to the exciting political displays that he eagerly attended in 1860. Daniel's father, an old Whig, joined other supporters of the Constitutional Union candidates John Bell and Edward Everett in wearing little gold or silver bells on their watch chains. Their parades featured floats with giant bells and processions lit by candles covered with paper screens, which lent a colorful aura to the occasion. But nothing could match the discipline and effect of the Wide-Awakes in the Republican parade, whose appearance "was as much a surprise to the crowd as was the sudden presence of the fearsome comet." In their light blue oilcloth capes and caps, carrying kerosene lamps at the end of wooden staffs, they projected confidence and determination; "they did not shout like the other men, but marched like trained troops to the music of fifes and drums." Daniel's mother turned to him as they passed and said, "Danny, I want you to remember them, because they mean a great change in history." The biggest surprise came when a float rolled by featuring a young man splitting rails—who turned out to be Daniel's older brother Frank, grinning at his Bell and Everett family![27]

Mrs. Beard's comment may seem a little too convenient in light of the events that followed the Republican victory and did, indeed, change history. But Daniel had another tale of a political event that his mother wanted him to remember. After his election, Lincoln visited Cincinnati, where he stood in an open carriage, waving and shaking hands with people lining the street. Daniel's mother told his aunt they would take the boys to see the president, "after which we will give them both a sound whipping!" When her sister asked why in the world they would do such a thing, she said, "the appearance of this man Lincoln marks a historical event of the gravest importance to America and the world, and if we whip the boys they will never forget seeing him." The whipping never took place, but Daniel managed to remember the day clearly. No doubt like countless thousands of other children from that time, he recalled that, as he ran alongside the carriage in which Lincoln rode, the president-elect turned to him and smiled. Suddenly, Daniel realized that his father—who had voted against Lincoln—had made a terrible mistake. "How could anyone vote against the great Lincoln? I was vaguely conscious even then that this man had the foresight of a prophet, a vision as broad as the prairies, and the brooking wisdom of the forest." And, matching perfectly Beard's later work with the Boy Scouts, he declared, "Lincoln possessed the natural, unconscious democracy of an outdoor man, which scattered the dry leaves of dead political theories in every direction."[28]

Not all parents wanted their children to be so deeply engaged in prewar issues. Richard Henry Dana and his wife discouraged their daughter Henrietta, born in 1856, from reading the second volume of *Uncle Tom's Cabin* by conveniently "misplacing" it, even though Harriet Beecher Stowe was a dear friend of Mrs. Dana's and a favorite of the Dana children. Years later Henrietta admitted that the "lurid stories of Cassie and Legree, and the martyrdom of poor Uncle Tom" were "rather strong meat" for a child.[29]

Once the war began, though, the "meat" of the political debates, war news, and public displays grew even stronger. Nevertheless, as they had before the war, Northern children gladly fulfilled their roles in the larger communities where they lived.

Families

The antebellum North had seen the beginning of a dramatic transformation in the dynamics of families, especially in the middle and upper classes. Although American mothers and fathers had always loved their offspring, the emotional satisfaction of raising children came to overshadow completely its economic benefits. As more Americans lived in urban areas, family size declined, and the growing economy rewarded many Americans with the affluence necessary to create the "child-centered" families more familiar to modern Americans. Simply put, children became more precious to their parents. Parents gave their children unique names (rather than the names of family members or previously born but deceased siblings), celebrated their birthdays, bought them commercially produced games, toys, and books, and encouraged them to call them Mama, Papa, or other affectionate and informal names. The middle classes also chose to produce fewer children, increasing the emotional value of each individual child. And because most middle-class women became separated from the economic sphere, the industrializing and urbanizing economy—and the development of the so-called cult of true motherhood—allowed them to lavish their energy on their children, to find a sense of purpose and to locate feelings of self-worth in their roles as mothers, leading them not only to accept rather romantic notions of childhood innocence and docility but also to devote ever-increasing resources, reflected in more toys and books and education, to their ever-shrinking families.[30]

This shift in attitudes toward families and childhood gained power from American industrialization. Its developing economic institutions, retail outlets, marketing and transportation companies, and other nonindustrial activities created the need for a large white-collar labor pool. Engineers, managers, bookkeepers, accountants, architects, lawyers, salesmen, clerks, typists, personal secretaries, and countless other virtually new occupations employed thousands of white men, whose relatively high salaries financed a very different lifestyle for their wives and families. Released from farm work and from many household chores—even middle-class families could afford servants in the labor market of the nineteenth century—wives and children enjoyed freedom and comforts unimaginable to most of the population who remained a part of the working class.

Many children still had to work, of course, especially on the farms that still dominated the antebellum Northern economy. Although the work of farm children in many ways varied according to age and gender, the responsibilities were not etched in stone. Strength rather than age tended to determine whether a boy could wield an axe or swing a scythe, and availability rather than gender tended to determine whether girls were expected to work in the field. If, for instance, a farmer had no sons but five daughters, it was extremely likely that those girls would end up doing a fair number of "boy" chores. Emergencies—a hard frost, a late harvest season, injuries to fathers and older brothers—could always force women, girls, and small children into the fields. Normally, however, there was a separation of labor. Boys followed their fathers into the fields and helped with the livestock; girls stayed closer to the house, performing household chores but also caring for chickens and processing the milk into cream and butter. The work performed by women and girls could account for a huge percentage of farm income; on the average Northeastern farm in 1860, for instance, dairy products, processed poultry, and eggs provided $630 in income; crops, livestock, and other farm products produced $783—and that included garden and orchard production, with which women and girls were no doubt intimately involved. Children could perform many valuable tasks on the average farm in a developed area: they fed and cleaned livestock, tended gardens, churned butter, collected sap for maple sugar, shelled corn—the list of possible ways to spend their time in hard labor must have seemed endless to children.

Yet the lives of farm children were being changed by a number of forces acting upon the agricultural economy. Mechanization, of course, had made farm work somewhat easier; mechanical planters, reapers, and rakes made it possible to farm more land with less sweat. Thus farm families needed fewer children to work on the farm. At the same time, however, those children became more valuable because they were able to perform a larger proportion of the necessary work, which needed less muscle and less skill to complete. Only a full-grown, experienced man could spend a day scything a field of hay or grain, or broadcast seed evenly over many acres of plowed field. As more of the skilled, heavy-duty farm jobs were done by machines, children became, in the words of one historian, "more productive (valuable), yet less essential."[31]

Other children, in small towns and cities, also entered the workplace. Family requirements influenced the work lives of many youngsters, and there is some evidence that not all autobiographers who reflected on the supposed character-building of childhood labor felt particularly empowered by their parents' decision to put them to work. One Vermont boy, the son of a Methodist minister, had attended a few weeks of school each year, but when he reached the age of fourteen "it was decided that . . . I must forego further attendance at school and secure a job of some sort." He ended up working on an upstate farm and apparently liked it, but his use of the passive verb—"it was decided"—suggests that it was not his choice to begin a life of work.[32]

A Massachusetts boy named John Albee worked through most of his fatherless childhood, his many and varied jobs interspersed with erratic episodes of formal education. Apprenticed at the age of eight to a bootmaker and at the age of ten to a sawmill, he later spent time making boots with his mother and sister, working as a shop boy, and manufacturing pistols before finally working his way through a couple of precious years at Worcester Academy with janitorial work and by delivering newspapers. After a brief career as a schoolmaster and a short stay at Harvard, he went into business.[33]

While boys could frequently expect to do a very different kind of work as adults than they were obliged to do at home—few farm or household chores were related to blue- or white-collar work—girls who grew up to join the work force performed jobs closely related to their childhood activities. A girl growing up in a house without servants frequently became a domestic herself. In the 1820s and 1830s, traditional New England home crafts like spinning and weaving were transported into factories—and many young women followed. The nurturing component of women's lives, which many girls learned as older siblings of young children, could be transferred into careers as teachers. The transition into the nonhousehold economy could be liberating, as studies of the famous "Lowell girls" have

shown. Young women—many of them teenagers and, by most defi-
nitions, still children—earned and spent their own money, enjoyed
friendships with other women and men outside their families and
hometowns, and explored cultural and social activities with gusto. A
higher percentage of college-educated women who became teachers
never married, as their economic opportunities gave them the option
to remain single. By the same token, entering the larger economy
could also create a deep sense of insecurity, for women cut off from
traditional dependence on men could easily slip into marginal economic circumstances. Even the traditional "hired girl" became a "domestic," with important distinctions. In the former case the "girl" in
question was usually the daughter of a neighbor or even a relative
hired for a limited length of time, who lived with the family employ-
ing her. In the latter case the servant was no more than an employee,
not a friend of the family, and the hierarchical character of the
employer/servant relationship, the low pay and long hours, created a
very different and not especially positive set of circumstances.[34]

So it was that while attitudes about children softened and expanded, the lives of many remained rooted in traditional economic
patterns. Both aspects of children's lives were touched by the Civil
War. And the ways Americans thought about families were enhanced by wartime strains and fathers' absences. Finally, while
many—probably a majority—of Northern children still contributed
to family economies on the eve of the Civil War, thousands more
went to work during the conflict to replace fathers and brothers
who had left for the army. Their labor not only fulfilled an obliga-
tion to their families but contributed to the war effort, transforming
their toil into a mark of patriotism. In these major and in a myriad
of minor ways, the Civil War had lasting effects on Northern children, their families, and the institutions that shaped their lives.

CHAPTER TWO

The War Culture and Northern Children

🖋 NORTHERNERS who grew up during the Civil War filled their memoirs with images of the war. They remembered collecting Confederate paper money, seeing young girls, including Gen. Ulysses S. Grant's daughter Nellie, portraying "the old woman who lived in a shoe" at fund-raising fairs, watching companies and regiments march off to the front or to assembly points, witnessing dramatic political debates, visiting training camps near major towns and cities to see relatives or bring supplies, waiting with friends and neighbors outside telegraph or newspaper offices for the latest news from the front, feeling a little awestruck when returning soldiers—especially wounded veterans—passed through their towns, poring over the battlefield maps and war-related articles that dominated the newspapers each morning. Toddlers learned patriotic songs and, as in the famous painting by Lilly Martin Spencer called "The War Spirit at Home," celebrated the news of Yankee victories.

A little girl living in Nantucket recalled as an adult how the war culture had entered her life. She would lie on the floor, "just absorbed in worship," as she looked at a colored lithograph of Elmer Ellsworth, the dynamic young officer killed early in the summer of

1861. She and other children and adults would gather at the town pier waiting for the ferry to bring the latest newspapers. She made those older girls in town who had beaus in the military into heroines in their own right; some proudly wore the badges of the corps to which their boyfriends and fiancés belonged. She also recalled more frightening images, when torchlight processions climaxed with the burning of "terrible straw men, 'effigies' they were called," of one Confederate or another. "These nights were horrors"—but horrors she was strangely drawn to, and sometimes her mother would reluctantly let her accompany her brother to the bonfires.[1]

This mixture of attraction and repulsion characterized many Northern children's responses to the war. Few elements of Northerners' lives remained untouched by the war, and though Yankee civilians rarely had to confront invading armies or extreme privation, their lives were nevertheless infused by a vibrant war culture. Perhaps the most common experience of Northern children during the conflict was their often avid participation in that culture.

Darkening Shadows

At one level many Northern children—if they or their parents so desired—could maintain a certain detachment from the war. A few surviving diaries suggest that the war barely dented their writers' consciousness. In an otherwise admirably detailed diary of life on an upstate New York farm, a twelve-year-old boy fails to mention the war at all, while a teenage girl attending a boarding school in another part of the state remarks briefly only on the election of 1864, ignoring entirely the dramatic events of the last fall and winter of the war. Once the excitement sparked by the outbreak of war calmed, recalled Henrietta Dana, neighbor and classmate of the children of Henry Wadsworth Longfellow, "we children soon fell back into the gentle tenor of our pleasant school life" in Craigie

House, the Longfellow manse where a private tutor held forth. The Englishwoman was hired by the poet at least partly to keep the war's "shadows from darkening his children's minds."[2]

But most children refused to ignore the war. An unusual diary kept by a Boston boy—unusual for its detail and the author's age—suggests just how deeply the war reached into the Northern home front and how easily it was folded into this boy's life. Gerald Norcross, son of a prosperous merchant and Republican alderman, kept his diary throughout the war while he grew from a boy of seven to a preadolescent of eleven. It is primarily a chronicle of fun: trips and walks, books and games, toys and scrapbooks, snacks and parties, fireworks and kittens. Gerald was a busy little boy with a large circle of friends and an apparently endless supply of toys. His pastimes included baseball, hockey, ring toss, Old Maid, and marbles; playing with a toy village; and collecting autographs (and, like many small children, almost anything else that caught his eye). He was an enthusiastic reader who favored adventures, travelogues, and Jacob Abbott's "Rollo" books, the classic tales of a curious, good little boy learning the ways of the world in books like *Rollo Learning to Read, Rollo Learning to Work, Rollo's Travels*, and *Rollo's Philosophy*.

The war entered Gerald's world as another source of diversions and pastimes, and he integrated it seamlessly into his normal routine, adapting previous joys and occupations to the war. For instance, in addition to attending Goodwin and Wilbur's Circus, he also attended military parades, political rallies, the National Sailors Fair, and a rather disappointing display of the battle between the *USS Monitor* and the *CSS Virginia* in a huge pond set up on Boston Common. (Henry Cabot Lodge, who was slightly older at the time, "keenly enjoyed" the performance.) Gerald's collection of seashells and other curiosities, which numbered well over three hundred items by the end of the war, came to include a piece of army hardtack and a tiny pea-shooting cannon. Tucked into his reports of peaceful play were references to making army hats and playing with paper soldiers named for prominent Massachusetts officers. He and his friends continued their prewar group activities, such as fighting with Irish boys (not surprisingly, given his background, he called them "Micks"). But they also organized their own boys' company, which they called the Garibaldi Guards.[3]

Elsewhere in New England, a teenage girl living in Concord, New Hampshire, also found the war occupying more and more of her time. She continued attending school and dance class and various lectures and sermons, but as a resident of a state capital, home to politicians and headquarters to the state's war effort, she was also exposed to numerous events related to the war: talks on patriotism, "war meetings," a panorama on the "present war," dances hosted by regiments from the area, military funerals, benefit concerts, flag presentations, and a party celebrating the Emancipation Proclamation on January 1, 1863. She frequently went to the nearby training camp to listen to chaplains' sermons, deliver supplies, and visit friends, and she spent time raising money for the soldiers.[4]

Such war activities were, according to one of the boys of Dansville, New York, "great fun for the boys and we were always there." The youngsters were drawn to the fifes and drums playing near the army recruiting office and to the "awkward squads drilling on the public square." At war meetings "the band would play and fervid speeches by our most eloquent citizens be made"; as the war dragged on, bounties of increasing size were offered to hesitant recruits. At one meeting, he remembered, a young man publicly stated his interest in receiving the bounty worth several hundred dollars but hesitated because of his wife's concerns. Much to the delight of the boys in the crowd, a village wit yelled, "Don't let that worry you, young man, I'll take care of your widder." At another meeting a local man delivered an original, impassioned, and patriotic poem that ended with a call to "Go, strike the traitor down!" and with his sudden "whacking" of a little boy he had concealed behind him; the boy collapsed, symbolizing the imminent fall of the

AFTER THE WAR:
Everything & Everybody en militaire

Outdoor scene :- Corner of Bombshell and Barrack Avenues

Interior The Piano superseded by the Big-Drum

The Central Park : Carriages, toys, etc. en militaire

A wartime cartoon found humor in the warlike culture that developed in the North. (*Harper's New Monthly Magazine, April 1862*)

Confederacy. A more serious and inevitable feature of war culture came to the Dansville boys when a local hero, a colonel, was buried with full military honors in the local cemetery. The boys witnessed "the solemn procession marching to the beat of muffled drums with the war-horse led behind the hearse." Scenes like these, which took place throughout the North during the war, made for "solemn times" whose "influence was felt keenly by the boys through those long four years."[5]

Little girls felt the same influence. A Wisconsin woman recalled the thrill of being carried down the street by her soldier-cousin when he came home on furlough and of sitting on a fence with a gaggle of children and shouting, "Vicksburg is taken! Vicksburg is taken!" Listening to the war talk that dominated public gatherings and family conversations, "we absorbed the spirit of the North and hated the South." Even lullabies were given over to sad war songs like "The Vacant Chair":

> We shall meet, but we shall miss him,
> There will be one vacant chair;
> We shall linger to caress him
> When we breathe our evening prayer.

She recalled years later, "We children caught the spirit of the times, though but dimly comprehending what it was all about."[6]

Your Country Calls

Perhaps nothing better illustrates the development of a war culture in the Northern states than the fact that valentines, a quite recent product of the sentimentalization of Victorian courtship, adopted warlike images. Although not necessarily intended for children, a number of valentines featured war-related themes. On one, a paper tent flap opened to reveal a soldier at a writing table with a vision of a young woman floating above him. Below, framed in a rectangle of roses, was the verse "Love Protects":

> Strong is the warrior's arm,
> That strikes for fortune and Fame,
> Thrice armed his stalwart form,
> Who fights in thy dear name.

The envelope depicted a couple standing in a crowded Victorian parlor, looking deeply into each other's eyes, with a cupid giggling in the background.

War culture could sometimes carry a lighter touch, as in another card that made fun of men who escaped military service by enlisting in the home guard. Featuring a cartoon of a man in an exaggerated prewar militia outfit, with outsized gun and sword, the verse read:

> You've heard, no doubt, of "carpet knights,"
> And one of those I guess you are, sir,
> Whom mere hen-hussy-work delights
> Much more than going to the war, sir!
> Your country calls, sir;
> Why hang back?
> Your arm might help the good cause, maybe,
> Then draw your sword the foe to whack,
> And let the *women tend the baby*.[7]

A similarly lighthearted approach surfaced in wartime jokes that made the rounds, often based on wordplay and puns. A thirteen-year-old New Yorker recorded a cousin's skit, minstrel style, that drew on Gen. George B. McClellan's disastrous campaign on the Virginia peninsula during the spring and summer of 1862. "Julius" informs "Mr. Johnson" that he had "seen the largest room in the world." "Why where was it?" asks Johnson. "Down on the Rappahannock. What room down there? Why the room for improvement.

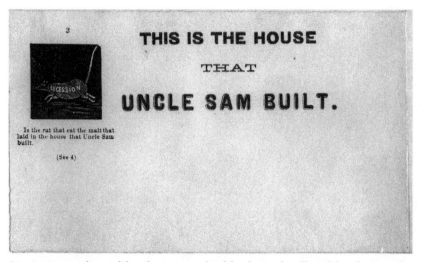

Patriotic envelopes like these were highly desired collectibles during the war. *(Wilson Library, University of North Carolina at Chapel Hill)*

How do you make it a room for improvement? Just send little Mac down there."[8]

Children's rhymes and songs were also mobilized for the war. "Paddy-cake, paddy-cake, baker man" became "Scott's Reveille" (after Gen. Winfield Scott, commander of Union forces at the beginning of the war):

> Rub-a-dub, rub-a-dub, this is my plan,
> I'll master the rebels as fast as I can;
> Catch 'em, and whip 'em, and mark 'em with a T,
> And hang all the leaders, as soon you shall see.[9]

Yet another borrowing of children's culture on behalf of the war effort was "This Is the House That Uncle Sam Built," a revision of "This Is the House That Jack Built," which appeared on a series of envelopes published in the North and was collected by adults and youth alike. Popular in both the Union and the Confederacy, most examples of this patriotic stationery were illustrated with flags, sol-

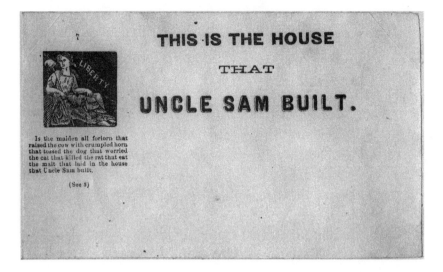

diers, and other patriotic emblems in the upper left-hand corner of the envelope, though some included satiric poems, mottoes, and cartoons. Indeed, one Northern boy recalled that "a really good history of the War between the states" could be drawn from the patriotic stationery published during the war. But a series of ten envelopes adapted the repetitive children's tale to the sectional crisis. Although most of the words were unchanged, the small cartoons that accompanied them and a few substitutions of phrases and names told the story of the secession of the Confederacy and the North's determination to save the Union:

> The house that "UNCLE SAM" built [the U.S. Capitol]. This is the malt [a bag of grain labeled "the blessing we have enjoyed as one people"] that laid in the house that Uncle Sam built. SECESSION is the rat that ate the malt that laid in the house that Uncle Sam built. OUR UNION PRESERVED is the cat that will kill the rat that ate the malt that laid in the house that Uncle Sam built. Davis is the DOG that worried the cat that will kill the rat that ate the malt that

laid in the house that Uncle Sam built. SCOTT [Gen. Winfield Scott] is the cow with the crumpled horn that will toss the dog that worried the cat that will kill the rat that ate the malt that laid in the house that Uncle Sam built. LIBERTY is the maiden all forlorn that raised the cow with the crumpled horn that will toss the dog that worried the cat that will kill the rat that ate the malt that laid in the house that Uncle Sam built. UNCLE SAM is the man all tattered and torn who married the maiden all forlorn who raised the cow with the crumpled horn that will toss the dog that worried the cat that will kill the rat that ate the malt that laid in the house that Uncle Sam built. This is the Parson now dead and gone [George Washington] that married the man all tattered and torn to the maiden all forlorn who raised the cow with the crumpled horn that will toss the dog that worried the cat that will kill the rat that ate the malt that laid in the house that Uncle Sam built.[10]

Although none of these bits of martial ephemera was necessarily intended for children, young Northerners nevertheless added patriotic envelopes to their collections of war souvenirs, recorded the jokes about generals and politicians in their journals, and, like Gerald Norcross, exchanged military-themed valentines. Their nascent patriotism and their natural inclination to take part in the excitement around them caused Northern boys and girls to embrace the war culture and to feel they had a role to play in the great events of the day.

Faithful and Comprehensive Histories

Throughout the war, Civil War entertainments filled Northern theaters, enticing children and their parents to view paintings and reenactments of battles, listen to martial music, and applaud patriotic speeches and plays. One young New Yorker joined a throng of excited spectators at the Academy of Music to watch an exhibition of how casualties would be picked up and transported from the battlefield. The exhibition literally began with a bang, with a "representation of a desperate combat, with its rattle of musketry and boom of heavy artillery and glare of red fire and clouds of copiously produced and highly pervasive battle smoke." As the smoke drifted out over the audience, a brace of "new, improved" ambulances rolled onto the stage and a squad of stretcher bearers leaped into action, picked up the blue- and grey-clad figures strewn on the stage, and placed them in the ambulances. "In less time than it takes for the telling the battle stage was cleared of its welter."[11]

Panoramas were the most dramatic of the entertainment options presented to Yankee children (who were always admitted at reduced prices). Following in the tradition of antebellum panoramas, which tended to feature travelogues, exotic locations, and striking scenes of action and conflict, entrepreneurs gave their panoramas fantastic names and enhanced them with dramatic narratives and musical accompaniments. Stanley and Conant's "Polemorama! Or, Gigantic Illustrations of the War" appeared for a long run at Tremont Temple in Boston during the late summer and fall of 1862. The sixty separate paintings depicted the first year or so of the war, beginning with landscapes of the principal locations, from Washington, D.C., to Charleston Harbor. Subsequent panels featured the bombardment of Fort Sumter, the attack on the Sixth Massachusetts as it passed through Baltimore, the destruction of the federal navy yard at Norfolk, Virginia, and U.S. troops marching into Virginia over the Long Bridge spanning the Potomac River near Washington. The second section featured the campaign in western Virginia and battles (now nearly forgotten but in 1861 headline-grabbing) like Romney, Laurel Hill, and Rich Mountain, as well as two panels from the defeat at Bull Run, including the Union army's disorderly retreat from the battlefield. A separate block of illustrations showed the lives of slaves in the South as well as their escape to Union lines at

Fortress Monroe; Gen. Ambrose Burnside's successful occupation of a corner of coastal North Carolina in early 1862; and the campaigns in Missouri (Wilson's Creek), Tennessee (Fort Donelson), and Arkansas (Pea Ridge). The series climaxed with "Scenes on the Peninsula," which gave rather short shrift to the massive and extended campaign that temporarily threatened the Confederate capital at Richmond in the summer of 1862; the decidedly misleading final panel depicted "The Rout of the Rebels" (in fact, after days of heavy fighting, the Union army was forced to pull back).

Advertising for the wartime panoramas resembled prewar promotions for museums and other supposedly wholesome entertainments. The "Polemorama" was "decidedly the best exhibition of the kind ever given in the city of Boston," that would provide "a more vivid idea of the great struggle in which our country is engaged" than "months of reading." Such glowing discussions may have encouraged parents to bring their children; youngsters would have been drawn to the comic relief provided by a fictional character inserted into the story. Panel sixteen introduced "our special artist," who in subsequent pictures led the panic at Bull Run, was captured by the Confederates in North Carolina, and later escaped. The comedy was enhanced by the songs played as accompaniment to his scenes: "Oh, Dear, What Can the Matter Be?" and "The Rogue's March" (when he was tarred and feathered for some unexplained violation of military protocol).[12]

Public celebrations of Independence Day took on added emotion during the war, when Northerners feared that the independence won four-score years ago might be ruined by the South's secession. In 1862 Bostonians pulled out all the stops, hanging flags and bunting from houses and trees, displaying banners pledging allegiance to the Constitution, and, in a nod toward the old days of the Revolution, erecting a "Liberty Pole" on Boston Common. Cadet militias from city schools joined soldiers on parade, and hundreds of schoolchildren sang "Old Glory" at the Academy of Music.

Along with these patriotic spectacles, children and adults alike watched a sailing regatta on the Charles River, magic tricks at Tremont Temple, and a balloon ascension from the Common.[13]

Surrounded by dramatic and inspirational images, children inevitably reenacted the political and military spectacles of the day. A family of Iowa children would go with their father to Republican meetings, then recreate the speeches and songs for their mother. A youngster in Connecticut, captivated by the big-screen panoramas, made his own version from illustrations cut out of *Harper's Weekly*. Colored, pasted together, and rolled onto a wooden spool, the pictures became a pint-sized panorama that the boy showed to friends and relatives, complete with a stirring narration. Charles, the older brother of future actor Otis Skinner, "organized a company of boys and girls, wrote and produced plays, war plays inspired by the conflict of the North and South." A wide variety of characters, from soldiers and sailors to planters and slaves, "formed the characters in Charlie's tragedies which were given in our cellar kitchen," where the young entertainer had chalked scenes on the walls. "Properties were few and poor, but our imaginations were rich": a packing case became a cell at Libby Prison, "a board tilted on a saw-horse" became Seminary Ridge, empty barrels became cotton presses, and washtubs turned into gunboats.[14]

Schools became important sources of patriotic imagery and socialization. One New Yorker recalled that "patriotism was pumped into" his schoolmates through the daily singing of a large repertoire of war songs, including "The Star-Spangled Banner," "Battle Hymn of the Republic," and "Marching Through Georgia." School administrators put boys—and sometimes girls—through military drills, and teachers organized patriotic pageants. Weekly "speaking days," a traditional feature of antebellum education designed to teach students elocution and appreciation for public speaking, became another conduit for patriotic displays, as did graduation ceremonies. Coached to speak in certain ways and to make specific gestures to indicate different emotions, students delivered excerpts from famous speeches, poetry, and other bits of literature and public pronouncements. Dramatic pieces like "Barbara Frietchie" and "Sheridan's Ride," tearjerkers like "Home News in Battle-Time," and political addresses by Daniel Webster and Abraham Lincoln were popular sources of inspiration. This is not to say that all Northern children marched in lockstep to a Republican version of patriotism. A speaking day at the end of the school year of the Boston Public Latin School deteriorated into giggles and snide comments as Democratic-leaning boys delivered what one boy called "old worn-out pieces" for laughs—and got them. By the end of the hour, even the "Battle of Hymn of the Republic" failed to quiet the young rowdies, who laughed all the way through it.[15]

Still, in many schools politics ran hot enough to cause fistfights and feuds, especially in communities where the Republican and Democratic parties were fairly equally represented. A Baltimore orphanage was seized by a "warlike spirit" that brought bickering and wrestling to every recess, while a Minnesotan remembered with relish the power that lay behind such epithets as "Rebel," "Copperhead," and "Black Republican," as well as the "certainty of being able at any minute to stir up a fight simply by marching up and down aggressively" and singing that favorite wartime anthem of children, "We'll Hang Jeff Davis on a Sour Apple Tree." A brawl broke out in a Chicago high school when sons of local Democrats threw the Republican name for them—"Copperheads"—back in the faces of their tormenters by wearing copper pennies as badges. A similar practice led to a months-long conflict in Dayton, Ohio, between "Union leaguers" (wearing Yankee uniform buttons) and "Butternuts" (another nickname for Confederates, represented by pins made of halved walnut shells). Dayton happened to be the hometown and center of support of Clement Vallandigham, the longtime congressman who was so vocal in his opposition to the war and to Republican war aims that in 1863 he was banished to the

Confederacy. By that time the conflict in the schools had escalated into fistfights and stone throwing. Unionist students organized clubs to protest the wearing of "butternut" badges, newspaper editors clashed over the proper treatment of the students, and school administrators vainly tried to end the disruptions by barring the wearing of any badges to school. The controversy waned when Vallandigham was arrested and removed from town. In Maryland, a state notably divided in its political opinion, the Baltimore city council required teachers to swear a loyalty oath, but a number refused to do so.[16]

Another, more subtle effect of the war appeared in schoolbooks published during the war. Although Northern publishers did not make nearly as much of an effort to integrate the war into textbooks as did Southern publishers, who produced dozens of textbooks with names like the *Dixie Primer* and *Confederate Reader*, martial images, war-inspired stories, and even a few math problems with military contexts did appear in Northern classrooms by the end of the war. One arithmetic book asked students to add up the number of Massachusetts men serving in the Union army and the quantity of uniforms, shoes, and hats produced for the army by Massachusetts factories; to figure out the percentage of an army made up of cavalry and infantry; and to make various calculations related to military garrisons, battle casualties, and marches.[17]

Several texts mentioned warfare in generic terms; *Willson's Primary Speller*, for example, asked its users to learn a few words and phrases related to conflict. *Battle, warfare, mortal wound, besiege, garrison,* and *brigadier* were just a few. By the end of the war, another spelling book had incorporated much more ambitious words, ranging from *reconnoiter* and *rebellion* to *belligerent* and *guerrilla, traitorous* and *contraband, stratagem* and *ambuscade, embrasure* and *commissary*.[18]

Not all mentions of war were positive. The *National Fourth Reader* contained an essay called "War" which, though not specifically about the conflict raging in the United States, cast an extremely negative light on any war, which its author called "the triumph of Death." The images could not have been comforting to students whose father and brothers were serving their country. Soldiers who died in battle, the piece asserted, were the lucky ones, "since they are exempt from those lingering diseases and slow torments to which others are liable." After a battle, thousands of soldiers were left to die on the battlefield, "their wounds exposed to the piercing air, while the blood, freezing as it flows, binds them to the earth, amid the trampling of horses, and the insults of an enraged foe!" Even un-wounded soldiers suffered from their rough diet, exposure to weather, and the stultifying existence of camp, where the "ravages of disease exceed those of the enemy." Finally, no one was safe, even those living on the home front. The enemy might appear on "the streets, where no sounds were heard but those of peaceful industry, filled of a sudden with slaughter and blood. . . . The houses of the rich pillaged, and every age, sex, and rank, mingled in promiscuous massacre and ruin!"[19]

Few schoolbooks presented war so realistically. G. S. Hillard's *Sixth Reader*, published after the war, included fairly standard modern pieces like Daniel Webster's attack on the slave trade and his defense of the Union, as well as Oliver Wendell Holmes's poem "Union and Liberty," Lincoln's "Gettysburg Address," and Thomas Buchanan Read's heroic "Sheridan's Ride." Yet among the classical selections was a piece by a Roman author known only as Athenaeum. The vivid images of his "The Contrast; or Peace and War" must have reminded the teenagers who used this book of the war so recently ended in their own country. As the first reading in the entire book, "Peace and War" set the tone. In times of peace, adults go about their work, children play on city fortifications, "law sits steady on her throne, and the sword is her servant." War descends on this tranquil scene, however, "like a water-spout, and deluges the land with blood." Farms and homes are burnt, livestock is driven away, "the temples are profaned; the soldier's curse resounds in the home of god," and "the golden cords of society are loosed." Hospitals fill with the maimed and diseased, young men become "more decrepit" than their grandfathers, and "everything unholy and unclean comes abroad from its lurking-place."[20]

Much more positive—not surprisingly, considering its title—was the tone of *The Patriotic Speaker*, issued in 1864. Although 80 percent of the entries in this sampler of speeches, articles, essays, poetry, and other literary items to be used to teach elocution were originally published before 1861, most related to issues and attitudes that any Union-loving Republican would feel comfortable with. The compiler acknowledged that many of the extracts were responses to students' requests for pieces "reflecting the great interests of the time." Many of the speeches were drawn from the great political debates over slavery, including several selections from William Henry Seward and Charles Sumner on slavery, the admission of Kansas, and the slave power. Other pro-Union speakers included Edward Everett and the abolitionists William Lloyd Garrison and Owen Lovejoy. A few disunionists and Copperheads also appeared, including Jefferson Davis and Clement Vallandigham. Most selections were fairly dry recitations of the strength of the American system, the importance of free speech, and the relevance of the U.S. Constitution. Included in the small selection of dramatic scenes was "Hush! Or the Grand Master of the K.G.C.," a reference to the Knights of the Golden Circle, an almost mythical antebellum organization that was purported to be plotting the invasion of Mexico and other countries south of the United States in order to expand the institution of slavery.[21]

As Mean as It Can Be

Unlike Southerners, who normally included the Reconstruction years in their memoirs of wartime, Northerners who had lived through the Civil War rarely extended their war recollections past the end of the fighting. Many punctuated their war stories with references to the death of President Lincoln. The grief and ceremony and sad excitement that followed the assassination became one last example of the war culture that infused children's lives.

"I have never met a man old enough to recall Lincoln's death," asserted one writer long after the war, "who did not remember precisely where he was and what he was doing." He himself was four, playing with an eight-year-old girl outside her father's saddle shop. For him, the most striking part of that long-ago moment was her understated, childlike, but entirely appropriate words: "I think it's just as mean as it can be." A woman who was very small in 1865 declared rather testily that "they said in the family that it was absurd—that I was too young—that I could not possibly remember the night Lincoln was shot." But, wrote Mary Adams French sixty years after the war, "I could, and I did." Mary and her parents were awakened by a policeman tapping on the bedroom window. When her father threw open the blinds, the officer cried, "President Lincoln assassinated! Dead! Seward stabbed!" The images of the next few days blurred over the decades between that morning and Mary's memoir, but she never forgot the striking scene of the policeman at her parents' window.[22]

It was unnerving for children to see their parents so upset and confused. For the first time in their lives, they saw grown men crying in public. When Anna Robertson's family drove into a nearby town on the fateful day, they knew something was wrong when they saw homes and shops decorated with black mourning bunting. When a storekeeper told her mother that the president had died, her mother cried, "Oh, what will become of us now?" The future journalist Ida Tarbell could never forget her normally calm mother "burying her face in her apron" and "running into her room sobbing as if her heart would break."[23]

There were, of course, rituals to be completed before the assassination—and the victim—could be laid to rest, and the hoopla surrounding the long journey of the president's body to Springfield, Illinois, provided another layer of wartime experience. The "Lincoln Special" included a locomotive boasting a large picture of the fallen leader, wreathed in garlands, on its cowcatcher. Thousands of people gathered on the streets to watch the coffin carried to and from government buildings, where it lay in state in a number of cities. Ten thousand people viewed the body in Baltimore, 300,000 in Philadelphia, and perhaps half a million in City Hall in New York City. The train crept halfway across the continent, viewed by huge crowds wherever it went. Even the smallest towns turned out in force to catch a glimpse of the car carrying their dead president. Frequently ribbons of black material arched over the tracks, placed there by mourners from nearby towns.

By the time Lincoln's body reached Chicago on May 2, 1865, nearly two weeks after leaving Washington, his skin had become discolored, upsetting some observers. A local undertaker applied rouge, chalk, and amber to restore the president's face to its natural hue. The deterioration in the cadaver's condition did not, however, stop Chicago from pulling out all the stops when it staged one of the biggest of the many funerals and memorial services held to honor Lincoln. Thirty-seven thousand people joined the funeral procession down Michigan Avenue, ten thousand schoolchildren wore black mourning sashes, and even Lincoln's horse, Old Bob, sported a black mourning blanket. Lincoln's coffin rested on a three-tiered, arched platform that cost $15,000 and was carried on a funeral carriage that featured a stuffed eagle on the roof and a team of ten horses decked out in mourning dress. The next day the train completed the last leg of the journey to Springfield, where the body was transported to the tomb in a gold, silver, and crystal hearse lent to Lincoln's hometown by the city of St. Louis.

Although children made up a large portion of the crowds lining streets and waiting in lines—one teenager spent an entire day, evening, and early morning making three trips past the casket in the U.S. capitol—they also found their own ways of processing their grief. On Nantucket Island the mother of nine-year-old Mary Starbuck returned from the local memorial service to find the first floor of their big old house decorated for the occasion. Mary and a friend had rummaged through Mrs. Starbuck's sewing bag and had hung black and white ribbons, garlands, ties, sashes, half-finished clothes, and rags from all the windows and doors that they could reach, in the little girls' version of an old-fashioned mourning custom. A group of teenage boys from Unionist families in Covington, Kentucky, donned their Sunday suits, pinned tintypes of the dead president edged with black cloth onto their lapels, and went around town ordering neighbors to close their blinds and attach to them black ribbons designating their grief.[24]

The music, book, and even toy industries also managed to add an assassination-tinged coda to the plethora of war-related artifacts produced during the previous four years. Within a few days of Lincoln's death, souvenirs and even toys appeared to commemorate the life and death of the sixteenth president. Predictably, the firm of Currier and Ives, which had spent the war producing wildly popular prints of military and other scenes of the war, published its own colored versions of the assassination, death, and funeral of President Lincoln. A number of pieces of sheet music were issued in the weeks after the assassination, ranging from William Willing's "The Flag Is at Halfmast: A Quartet," to a funeral march played at stops along the route of the funeral train, to "The Death Knell Is Tolling: A Requiem to the Memory of Our Late Beloved President Abraham Lincoln." One ballad that stood out in the crowded flurry of Lincoln songs and dirges was "The Assassin's Vision," which described the crime from the diabolical and doomed point of view of John Wilkes Booth. "As he hurried away from the scene of death, On his brow were looks of despair; Before him! Around him! The evening's breath, Told him God's vengeance was there!"

Indeed, the song ends oddly triumphantly; " 'Vengeance is mine!' saith God in his might."[25]

An unusually effusive and rather unique item was a children's puzzle made of twenty-four rectangular wooden blocks. Each featured four different images, which could be constructed into five different designs: a Children's Monument, a Freedman's Monument, and a National Monument, all to the slain president, a National Monument to George Washington, and a Presidential Monument. The Children's Monument included several illustrations: Lincoln's portrait, Lincoln reclining (apparently lying in state), and members of his family. But most of the blocks were filled with text, which began, "Great and immortal chieftain! Though cold and silent, thou art not dead," and went on to promise, "We are but children, yet thou hast a warm place in all our hearts. When our parents speak of the great and noble, they whisper thy name with reverence, and tell us to emulate thy virtues." It continued, "By patient, persevering toil, thou didst crush the viper treason, subdue the great rebellion, and give liberty to four millions of people," and concluded, "Thine shall be a fame sublime; And the virtues of thy soul; Shall, in triumph, onward roll, Until men and nations, free, Blend they name with LIBERTY." Cheap photographic prints of the conspirators, including their hooded bodies hanging from the gallows, were also popular in the weeks following the assassination.[26]

One family of children sought to exorcise its grief by falling back on one of its favorite pastimes. When Henry Wadsworth Longfellow's children and their playmate, Henrietta Dana, learned of the murder, they could hardly believe "that such a thing could ever happen in our civilized age, in our own free country, to our own good and dear President." But one of their favorite pastimes, a genre of war culture that had flourished during the previous four years, "came to our rescue," wrote Henrietta. "And as descriptions of the scene of the assassination began to appear in the daily papers and illustrated weeklies, with one heart and mind we rushed to stage the scene in our outdoor theater"—the east veranda of Craigie House.

It became the presidential box in Ford's Theatre, and the croquet lawn below became the stage on which the girls enacted scenes from "Our American Cousin," the play during which the murder had occurred. The older girls, more familiar with the facts of the tragedy and, it must be said, naturally condescending toward the younger girls, directed and took the best roles, while Henrietta, the youngest, got only "the dummy roles which no one else wanted." The tallest girl played Lincoln as he entered the presidential box, waving to the applauding audience, though Henrietta had to play Lincoln in the passive role of target and victim. The children played out the whole drama: the shooting, the stabbing of Major Rathbone, the leap onto the croquet lawn/stage—paper cutter in hand, shouting "*Sic semper tyrannis*"—the escape and chase, and the capture of Booth. The eight-year-old Henrietta had to act out the last moments of the "lonely, crippled, hunted fugitive" taking refuge in the stable at the rear of the house. The rest of the cast, playing the posse in hot pursuit, soon surrounded the hideaway; even Longfellow's "small fat Skye terrier" represented "a brace of manhunting bloodhounds." The posse shouted and jumped about, the dog barked, and Henrietta, overwhelmed with the scene and with her surprising empathy for the trapped criminal—"rather a lonely and even terrifying role for" an eight-year-old—was on the verge of tears. They played out the scene, however, and Henrietta's memoir went on to other topics, just as Americans had to move on to new phases in their lives.[27]

The war culture that infused the lives of Northern children was a superficial element of their war experiences. Boys and girls were eager consumers of entertainment, interested participants in patriotic school activities, and avid observers of all things related to the war. But they also faced far greater challenges and opportunities, and participated much more deeply in the home-front war effort. Although at times it may have been difficult to separate the war culture from the rest of their lives, the impact of the war on their families would prove to be more lasting and more important.

CHAPTER THREE

Family Life and the War

🖋 "DOWN TO THE OPENING of the war," recalled Maurice Egan of Philadelphia sixty years later, "our life at home had been a pleasant one." Sectional issues had lurked in the background, of course; Maurice's father was a dyed-in-the-wool Northern Democrat and a supporter of Stephen A. Douglas while his mother was an equally committed Southerner who believed that the Republicans planned to conquer the South and divide it up among the blacks living there. "The Northern Yankees would gladly consent to this," she assured Maurice, "as they were mere tradespeople who were jealous of the more cultivated population of the South." Maurice's political orientation was targeted by both parents, but especially his mother, who, after Mr. Egan left for work in the morning, would read aloud the speeches of the pro-Southern congressman from Ohio, Clement Vallandigham, which she considered to be "marvels of eloquence and truth." The tension grew worse as war approached: Mr. Egan became a moderate Republican after the election of Lincoln while Mrs. Egan "grew more and more enthusiastically Southern." For Maurice, "life began to be spoiled."

Politics had divided the extended family—"Our relatives all seemed to have quarrelled with us"—and Mr. and Mrs. Egan "became coolly polite to each other. There was very little gaiety, and finally they agreed not to mention the subject of politics to each other." Nevertheless, his mother continued to proselytize Maurice, but with unexpected results: the "violence" of her opinions "turned me toward the other side." Southern relatives sent them sheet music from the South—"The Bonnie Blue Flag" stuck out in Maurice's memory—but the neighborhood echoed with pianos (which just before the war had "begun to infest every home") pounding out the Union's "patriotic songs, good, bad and indifferent." Despite the presence of a good many families of Southern stock and of the pre-vailing Democratic leanings of most of the Northerners in Philadel-phia, Maurice and the other boys, "with a curious insight, seemed always to believe in Lincoln, no matter what their parents thought."[1]

The Civil War placed immense pressure on Northern families, jarring routines, heightening fears, and threatening the fabric of fam-ily life. Fathers and brothers went off to the army, separating families for months, years, and sometimes forever. Children's roles within families sometimes changed. Many children found themselves tak-ing on greater workloads and responsibilities. Some middle-class children worked harder than ever before while the labor of working-class children became even more important to their families than it had been before the war, as wives and children were forced to sustain family economies. Mothers' personalities sometimes changed be-cause of the pressure of work and childrearing, and many boys and girls had to grow up faster because of declining opportunities and rising hardships. Still, families tried to maintain peacetime routines and assumptions and fathers desperately attempted to retain their authority and affection for their children.

A Sad Day in Our Household

The most basic threat to families, of course, came when fathers and brothers joined the military. Although the Union cause cast the decision to leave in a glow of honor and patriotism, the departure of men for the front could also inspire a grief-tinged sense of helplessness. Young boys and girls noticed a change—or at least reflected on that change when they wrote their memoirs years later—in their mothers when husbands and older sons went off to war. As one woman whose father and brothers had left along with most of the other men in the community wrote, work and other family responsibilities were carried out "by despairing women whose hearts were with their men."[2]

For some families, the drumbeat of patriotism and the sense of honor that came with the enlistment and devoted service of family members could not temper the overwhelming sadness and anxiety that, not surprisingly, plagued many wives and mothers. Jeannette Gilder and her sisters assumed that Mrs. Gilder shared their excitement after watching their father and brother march off to war with their regiment. Although as an adult Jeannette understood that "it was a sad day in our household," at the time "we children did not realize all that it meant." To the girls it was a stirring, patriotic moment that made them proud of their family's important role in the war effort. "With flags flying and bayonets glistening in the sun, the soldiers marched past our house on the way to the train. We children hung over the fence and waved good-bye, shouting to those we knew as they passed us." Some of the men turned to smile, and when their father passed, "we waved and shouted to him but he looked straight ahead and made no sign"—the first indication that not everyone in the family was as thrilled as they were. After the regiment had turned a distant corner, trailing the band's rendition of "The Girl I Left Behind Me," the girls dashed upstairs, expecting to find their mother waving goodbye, eager to tell her about the strange behavior of their father. They were surprised to find that, rather than leaning out the window as they had assumed, she had closed the shutters and was lying on the bed. "She was not crying. Her eyes were dry and wide open, but they looked at us without seeing us," Jeannette recalled. The daughters seemed suddenly to realize the gravity of the situation: "The words that were on our lips were unspoken, we turned and went silently down stairs, leaving her alone with her grief."[3]

The memoirs of the future senator from Nebraska, George Norris, offer a painful account of how the war could affect family dynamics. As a small boy in Ohio, George was barely aware of the war raging to the south and east, but he was acutely aware of the tribulations faced by his family, which lost a father and an older brother in the span of a few months. Mrs. Norris took the death of her eldest son hardest. George remembered him as the opposite of his stern father: "buoyant, cheerful, and companionable," and, "as is so frequently the case of a son in a large family of girls, my mother seemed to lean upon him and to shower an extra measure of affection upon him." She was proud of his year-long attendance at college and became deeply worried, after the war began, that he would join the army. So worried was she that she "exact[ed] from him a promise not to enter the armed service," which "gave her a temporary peace of mind." Nevertheless John eventually could no longer "bear the spectacle of his friends marching off in uniform," and he enlisted. His mother waited anxiously for each day's mail for letters from John, and "treasured those letters more than any other possession," tying them up in red ribbons, storing them in a tin box, and occasionally taking them out to reread them. George believed years later that he "could understand John's struggle with himself" and how painful breaking his promise to his mother must have been. Indeed, the younger Norris thought it was John's "failure to keep his word to her that caused my mother's sharpest grief" when news came that John had died of wounds received during the Atlanta campaign. Fewer than four months later, Mr. Norris died, leaving eight children and a pregnant wife. George remembered from his childhood that he "never heard a song upon the lips of my mother. I never even heard her hum a tune. . . . The war ended, and the young men came back, but John slept in a soldier's grave in the blackened southern countryside. There were times when it seemed that the heartache over her son never would pass."[4]

Who Will Care for You Now?

Loss was a continuing theme for Civil War families. Songs, poems, and stories lent the idea of sacrifice a poignant glory, but such notions rang hollow to women and children facing the deaths of husbands, fathers, and siblings from wounds and disease. Inevitably, wartime literature for children often featured tough orphans whose fathers had been killed fighting for the Union, but even they could sometimes reveal the depths of the sorrow experienced by grieving family members. A typical tale of a boy's home-front contributions featured a scene in which a group of men gathers in a town's general store, where they discuss newspaper reports of the local regiment's brave charge during a recent bloody but victorious battle. News of casualties is sketchy, and the mostly old or infirm men hate the uncertainty. Even more they hate knowing that a certain officer—husband of a woman struggling to keep up with the bills and to raise to manhood a bright twelve-year-old named Edward (Ned for short)—has been confirmed among the dead. When Ned suddenly appears at the door to ask about the news, the men refuse to look him in the eye. The kindly butcher, Mr. Jenkins, finally begins to answer Ned's questions, sharing reports of the regiment's fine performance and of Ned's father's heroism in leading the men straight into a storm of Rebel fire. Ned shouts a cheer for the victory and for the regiment, but their voices stick in the throats of the worried fathers and neighbors.

When Ned asks, "Who's killed?" Mr. Jenkins hems and haws a bit: "There's reports, . . . but I don't know as it is best to give too much heed to them, until we get official reports." Ned persists in his question: "Who is reported dead?" Jenkins replies, "Well, lots of them. Tom Crane for one, and Silas Dewey for another. Peter Blunt is missing, and Dan McGray is not to be found." All served in Ned's father's company, and Ned wishes that letters with reliable reports would come soon. "There are many of us that will look for letters that will never come, I am afraid," sighs Jenkins. "Oh, this war is terrible for us that stay at home, as well as for those that go. There are my two boys, I have not heard a word yet, and may never, for all that I know." Ned turns to go, but finally one of the old men decides Ned must not be allowed to think his father is all right when they all know he has been killed. "Edward Randall," he calls bluntly, "there ain't no use in trying to make bad news good, 'cause you must know it some day. Your father was killed, shot to pieces; but he died gloriously, all say." The notion of glory flees immediately from Ned's brain: "The shriek which came from the boy no one that heard it ever forgot. . . . The look, the posture, the agony of that child" silences the rather callous old man and the rest of the men in the room.[5]

The war brought family sacrifices to life. Although most Americans of the time had been raised on a rather generically Protestant notion that sacrifice was a necessary, even noble, part of life, and that sudden death was always a possibility, Northern children often had their first personal encounter with the death of a loved one during the Civil War. Maggie Deland's beloved "Cousin Pidge," who was also her teacher, was newly married to a soldier whom the children called "Captain Don." Although little Maggie was rather oblivious to the worry that must have wracked her cousin's mind after Don went with his regiment to the front, she did capture the essence of what it meant to die when word came that Don had been killed in action—though his body was never found. Of course Maggie knew the word *dead* and "used it, with great cheerfulness" when she sang about hanging Jeff Davis from a sour apple tree. "We children were always delighted" when they found dead birds or other animals, so they could stage a funeral. "But now, when the grown people said Captain Don was dead, that was different. They looked solemn, and there wasn't any funeral."[6]

That the loss of scores of thousands of Northern men should inspire Yankee civilians, including children, to live better, more patriotic lives was made clear in children's magazines, which created a genre of stories and poems featuring the aftermath of soldiers' deaths. A representative sample is "The Soldier's Little Boy." In this heartrending poem, published in *The Little Pilgrim*, "Little Willie" lies dying of an unnamed disease. "Who will care for you now, mother?" he asks.

> The pain of leaving you here alone
> Is the sharpest pain I have;
> For I know you will never smile again,
> And no little boy will be nigh
> To wipe the tears on your cheek away,
> And whisper—'Dear mother, don't cry!'

This affecting passage gives way to pious Victorian sentimentality, exaggerated by the knowledge that the man of the little family has been killed at Antietam, leaving the little boy to fill that role in the household. "I did what I could . . . But my hands were young and weak." Despite his sorrow at leaving his mother alone, like a good Christian boy, he was "not afraid to die . . .

> For the fear of death is past;
> But mother—oh, mother, you must not grieve,
> We'll meet again by and by—.
> Where every tear shall be wiped away—
> Father, you, and I."[7]

Worn down by the burden of replacing his father in the family, Willie is a perfect example of how patriotism, family loyalty, and responsibility meshed in the crucible of war.

Duties of Children in the National Crisis

For Civil War children, the war provided an opportunity to be truly useful, to display the qualities of hard work and reliability and maturity that were the focus of much of the education and childrearing practices that shaped their lives. Children's literature from the war period was filled with examples of ways that children could take on responsibilities that would aid their families and, by extension, contribute to the ultimate success of the war effort. Their willingness to assume duties normally performed by fathers or older brothers, to tighten belts, to do with fewer toys and books, to bear up under the strain that war placed on families throughout the country, became their greatest contribution to saving the Union. A typical literary representation of a boy meeting his family's needs was "The House That Johnny Rented," a long story serialized over several months in *The Little Corporal.* Johnny is the twelve-year-old son of Pastor White, who, despite having an invalid wife and several younger children, joins the army as a chaplain, thus forcing his family to move out of the church parsonage. As the title suggests, Johnny finds an equally pleasant cottage at a good price, persevering in the face of unfriendly landlords and his own discouragement.[8]

Many other stories and books dealt with the intersection of family responsibilities and the war effort. In *Frank's Campaign,* an early effort by Horatio Alger that contains many elements of his more famous postwar books, the hero wins a school contest with a composition on "The Duties of Boys in the Present National Crisis." He gets a chance to put theory into practice when his father enlists. In fact both fifteen-year-old Frank and his father want to join the army, but Frank lives up to the sentiments of his winning essay: with so many men off in the army, "it becomes the duty of the boys to take their places as far as they are able to do. . . . If he does this voluntarily, and in the right spirit, he is just as patriotic as if he were a soldier in the field." Frank gives up his martial dreams, quits school, and takes over the family farm. After momentary doubts, Frank rebukes himself for being selfish: " 'The country needs him more even than we do,' he said to himself. 'It will be hard trial to have him go, but it is our duty.' "

Frank has to deal with a number of other crises along the way: he foils the scheme of a war profiteer who tries to foreclose the mortgage on the family farm (incidentally, Frank's father had refused the $150 bounty for enlisting); wins a bitter contest with the war profiteer's son in the election for captain of a home guard company; befriends a family of black refugees; and helps a mysterious stranger settle the score with the man (the war profiteer) who had ruined the stranger's father. In typical Horatio Alger style, everything turns out well in the end: Frank's administration of the farm pays off, the mortgage is met, and Frank's new friend pledges to put Frank through school as a reward, he says, of doing "your duty . . . at the sacrifice of your inclinations." Alger made the main point of the book clear in his preface: "The great struggle in which we are now engaged for the integrity of the Republic has imposed new duties and new responsibilities upon all classes of the people. This little volume is intended to show how boys can be of most effectual service in assisting to put down the Rebellion."[9]

Real-life boys and girls also experienced dramatic changes in their lives and found ways to do their duty. The effect of the Civil War on the work patterns of American children was somewhat predictable. As hundreds of thousands of men left fields and factories for the front, someone had to take their places. Boys filled in for absent fathers on farms from Maine to Missouri; girls learned to do chores and plow fields for the first time in their lives; women had to manage farms and plantations and shops. In the rural North, reported one autobiographer who grew up in New York during that time, "extravagant wages were paid for indifferent help when it could be obtained, and a growing boy, willing and apparently strong, did an amount of work that the boy of today, or the man either, in like circumstances, would not attempt to do." Partly because of the opportunity presented by the demand for labor, partly out of necessity, many teenagers went to work. More than 250 "boys" were employed in the Washington Arsenal as early as June 1861 while enrollment in Baltimore high schools plummeted when scores of boys chose jobs over schooling.[10]

One Northern boy complained that, though he was only twelve years old, because so many men in his neighborhood had gone off to war he had "to assume the work and responsibilities" of a grown man. Many other young Northerners had to do the same thing. As one Iowa mother wrote, "the whole responsibility" of keeping their farm running "rested with myself and the children"—a thirteen-year-old girl, an eight- and a ten-year-old boy, and a baby girl. "They were my only assistance and companions . . . and it was wonderful what enthusiasm and helpfulness those four dear children manifested all the time. They seemed enthused with the spirit of the times."[11]

Eddie Foy, later in life a famous comedian, was only five years old when the war began, and he had no clear memories of it until his family was directly affected. He recalled as an adult a "dim recollection of being held up . . . at the curb to see long lines of soldiers marching down streets . . . with flags waving and bands playing and crowds cheering, and it all seemed very fine." But everything changed when his father enlisted in 1862, leaving behind four young children. A few months later he was wounded and came home, but his injury became infected and he lost his mind, eventually dying in an insane asylum. Not long afterward, Eddie's two-year-old sister died; "there seemed to be no end to our troubles in those days." The three surviving children—Eddie and two older sisters—went to work to support the family. He first worked as a bootblack, then became an entertainer. His first job in show business was as sidekick to a wandering fiddler, who taught Eddie a kind of minstrel song that began,

> I'm happy little Ned,
> I earn my daily bread
> By doing shoes for white folks 'round this town.
> I was never known to shirk
> From any kind of work,
> At blacking boots there's none can take me down.

The Foy family survived on the coins tossed to Eddie on the streets and in the saloons of New York City, Brooklyn, and Jersey City.[12]

Children took the place of absent fathers in more ways than simple economics. In some cases the role reversal—children becoming heads of the household and caring for mothers and younger siblings—was almost complete. During the Sioux Indian uprising in Minnesota, Frank Rogers and his brother Fred armed themselves with a sword and pistol and stayed up all night; their mother recalled many years later that "I felt quite safe with two such brave little soldiers." Another boy who took charge in a crisis was Levi Keeler, whose mother became seriously ill. She later wrote to her husband that Levi "sat up with me all night and every little while he would ask Mother do you want anything, till one o-clock and then I could not stand it any longer so Levi went after the Doctor." In a phrase that showed how deeply family responsibilities could be changed by the war, Jane Keeler wrote, "Levi was my man." Levi was nine years old.[13]

I Will Always Feel an Interest

Just after Christmas 1863, Martha Glover, a black woman in Missouri, sent a heartrending letter to her soldier-husband. Admitting that "it seems like a long time since you left me," Martha wrote,

"I have had nothing but trouble since you left." Although Missouri remained in the Union, it was still a slave state, and Martha's owners had taken out their anger over her husband's enlistment on Martha and her children. "They abuse me because you went & say they will not take care of our children & do nothing but quarrel with me all the time and beat me scandalously the day before yesterday." The children missed him terribly; they "talk about you all the time." Swinging back and forth between anger and passion, Martha declared that "you ought not to left me in the fix I am in & all these little help-less children to take care of," but a few sentences later she wrote earnestly, "We want to see you worse than we ever did before." Just before closing "Farewell my dear husband," Martha advised, "You need not tell me to beg any more married men to go [to the army]. I see too much trouble to try to get any more into trouble too."[14]

Most soldiers realized that their absence was causing untold emotional and physical hardships for their families, and in their let-ters home they tried to explain their decision to leave while at the same time maintaining their roles as heads of family. The difficulty of their decisions to leave wives and children—and the guilt they clearly felt in not being home during times of crisis or joy—led them to explain carefully their choices and the need for their con-tinued absence. The fervor they displayed in their formal justifica-tions suggests that they were trying to convince themselves as much as their wives that they were doing the right thing.

Henry Hitchcock's wife asked him to write a letter explaining why he had accepted a commission late in the war, so "you could have it to show to our boy, from his father, hereafter." "The rea-son I wished to enter the service," Hitchcock wrote, "was simply that I could not stay at home and let other men do the fighting & run the risks while I was safely making money & enjoying the fruit of their toils." When he finally enlisted, "I was very sure that I should hereafter be able to respect myself for at least having tried to do my duty."[15]

A man did not have to be an officer to yield to the demands of honor. "It may be . . . my unfortunate lot to fall," an Indiana sergeant admitted in a letter written just before his unit marched south. "If so I desire that we may so live that we will Meete in a better Land Where there is no Rebbels nor traitors to mare the peace of the inhabitants." He had left his home and family "for pure motives to sustain . . . The Goverment of our fore Father. But if it should be that I do not Return I wish you to instruct My little Boy that I die a Marter to my country, without any simpathy for traitors." "It is a glorious country," wrote a Yankee from a Rhode Island training camp, "and *must* be preserved to our children." The previous generation had given it "to *us entire*, and *we* must give it to you, entire and you must give it as you receive it, to those who come after you."[16]

It is impossible to know how many Union soldiers were fathers, but it is safe to say that there were tens of thousands of men who left behind small children. Their letters to wives and sons and daughters provide windows into the ways that mid-century families functioned, not only while fathers were away but also before they had left home.

Fatherly expressions of sympathy and guilt and sorrow flowed from camp to home. Mitchell Thompson, too far away to give his four-year-old daughter Corry a hug when she bumped her head, could only write "that her Pa recollects very distinctly of getting just such a rap on the head very much in the same way" when he was a boy. The worst moments for military fathers came when death visited their families. Only a few months after leaving home, Henry Ankeny of the Fourth Iowa was shattered to learn that his daughter had died. "Oh Tina," he wrote to his wife, "I know where I ought to have been in this great trial of yours, and would to God I had never left you to bear so heavy a load of grief and sorrow alone."[17]

Soldiers yearned for the details of their children's lives, to read, in the words of one soldier, "their childish thoughts about themselves, papa and mama and all other subjects that enter their little brains." Most spouses obliged. An Iowan wrote her absent husband that their toddler Charlie "has no fever and runs around. He is a caution for fun." Soldier-fathers longed to share in the daily intimacies they had known in peacetime, and many men imagined having their children with them. When David Coon concocted a dish out of stewed dried apples, milk, sugar, and hardtack, he immediately thought of his four-year-old. "I don't know why," he wrote, "but I thought how Johnny would enjoy it if he would sit down with Pa and help eat it." A Yankee captain besieging Vicksburg created a virtual family circle by surrounding himself with photographs of his children while writing them a letter.[18]

Fathers liked to share details of camp life as way of reassuring their families that they were all right, but others also liked to titillate their children with details from battlefields that only they could tell youngsters eager to hear war news. One Yankee officer told his wife, "Tell [eight-year-old] Hamlin that he must be a good Son and I will tell him all about the big fight; how I seen a Shoe with a foot in, shot off by a Cannon Ball and lots more." Less cheerful was a report from a father who had just survived the Battle at Shiloh, where he saw the field "strewn with dead men and horses. . . . Some lay in heaps of four & five some with there heads arms and legs torne of, it is one of the most horrible sights, there is no one can give A description of it"—except, he might have added, their father, the traditional source of strange and interesting tales, however horrific.[19]

In addition to providing exciting details from the battlefield, most fathers continued to fulfill their paternal responsibility by offering advice on a wide range of issues and situations. A Maine mother wrote her husband that, among all the reasons she wished he were at home, one of the most important was to instill a little discipline in their toddler, "to make the little image behave, for I'm too lazy." Most fathers were more than willing to help. In peacetime they would have delivered this advice daily; in wartime they had to distribute it in rushes, in infrequent letters where the tone of voice

and gestures and immediacy that normal life gave relationships between fathers and children were absent. But fathers nevertheless
tried to make their wishes known, to do their duty, to impose their
vision of their children's character and futures on the sons and
daughters back home.[20]

David Coon left nine children at home when he went off to
fight. He wrote them that the best thing they could give him was "a
good report" from home—assurances that they were doing their
chores and minding their stepmother and finishing their schoolwork. But, like parents of any time, Coon was not above using his
own situation to shame a child who stepped out of her proper place.
After a long description of the hardships and dangers he faced in
camp and on the battlefield, Coon lectured his fourteen-year-old
daughter Emma that she needed to treat her stepmother more respectfully. "Oh, my dear daughter, your father may be lying dead
on the field of battle and you may not know it. . . . O, Emma,
Emma! How can you have the heart to go to dancing parties,
against your kind mother's wishes and advice and your own conscience and judgment? How can you add to my grief and trouble by
such a course?" His last words were a not so subtle reminder of the
importance of fatherly advice and of the sacrifices he had—and
might—make on her behalf: "I am sorry I can't write with ink, as I
perhaps may never write to you again."[21]

Not all fathers attempted to govern their daughters. "I don't
pretend to understand a girl or a woman," Lt. Col. James Goodnow
assured his wife Nancy. He went on to promise that he would never
advise Nancy on how to raise their little daughter Belle; he considered himself simply too ignorant to have any notions about bringing up females. But he had plenty to say about how to raise sons,
and from the time he left home late in 1862 until he resigned his
commission two years later, Goodnow maintained a remarkable
correspondence with his three sons back in Jefferson County, Indiana. Although his oldest, teenager Sam, received the longest and

most detailed letters, James often enclosed separate notes for Daniel, who was about nine, and for Johnny, who was three or four. Like nearly all Civil War fathers who had the resources, education, time, and inclination to write home, Goodnow filled his letters with love and advice.[22]

James Goodnow's letters to his three sons rarely referred to nursery rhymes; his correspondence usually offered straightforward bits of advice and manly affection. But he was committed to continuing his role as guide and comfort to his boys. "I want that you and I should be regular correspondents during my absence," he wrote to Sam in his first letter home. He urged him to "tell your mind freely" in weekly letters, to "tell me all about what you are doing—and all about your cares and troubles—and you may be Sure I will always feel an interest in whatever interests or affects you." Although Sam and Daniel both wrote frequent notes to their father, their letters have not survived. But the several dozen letters written by Goodnow to his sons matched the interests and needs of each son. As the oldest, Sam received most of the general news about Goodnow's unit, including information about his father's travels in Alabama and other parts of the Western theater, speculations about military strategy, and a detailed description of the only battle that Goodnow fought. More important were the pieces of fatherly advice and compassion and affection that Goodnow freely distributed. His letters to Sam frequently, if gently, nudged him toward adulthood. "It will not be long before you will have to go out in the world to make your own way," he wrote in that first letter, "and you will then be too busy to study." He urged him to work hard at school, for "your success and usefulness will altogether depend on the way you employ your time now." Sam was also to "Remember always that your Mother has a right to your help" and that he could "never do too much for her."[23]

The mindful father often directed the boys to obey their mother. On one occasion he was uncharacteristically stern when he blamed Nancy Goodnow's poor health at least partly on the fact that "you have made her do too much work." Sam must realize how hard she had labored to care for him over the years and out of "common gratitude make up to her for what She has done for you." He and his brothers were to carry all the wood, make all the fires, milk the cow, work in the garden, help with the wash, and generally "take all work off her hands that you can do."[24]

Variations on these themes abounded. Although he expressed surprise that Sam had been temporarily suspended from school—he could not "believe you were deserving of such harsh treatment"— he advised him to go to the teacher, apologize, and promise to obey him in the future. "If he is a reasonable man that will be enough." Ever watchful of his son's future, Goodnow wrote that, as he approached manhood, Sam must learn to value the "habits of industry and also to . . . not be ashamed of honest labor." Apparently the young man was working while he attended school, which pleased his father, who commented that even if Sam did not care for the job, he could at least have "the Satisfaction of knowing that you are earning your own livelihood."[25]

The two younger sons received similar messages tailored to their ages and interests. Goodnow's first letter to "Master Daniel Goodnow" began with chitchat about Christmas, but he quickly moved to more exciting information regarding his army experiences. "Well Dan," he wrote breezily, "you ought to be out here and See our big armies." He described his army on the march out of Memphis and in camp. "If you would have been there you would have thought there was going to be a battle there was So much noise. The men Cheered and yelled and the mules brayed loud enough to make you jump out of your boots." Despite the excitement and drama, Goodnow was glad that his boys were not with him, "for wherever the large armies go here they drive the people away from home and take all they have to eat and all their corn and then burn their houses and fields—and a great many little boys down here do not have enough to Eat and often have no home." Dan also received advice, but of a very different sort from Sam. Whenever Dan felt like quarreling or crying, suggested Goodnow, "just run out into the wood Shed and Saw a few Sticks of wood and See if you don't get in a good humor before you get done." Even Johnny, whose mother had to read his letters for him, got advice. "I have been wanting to See you for a long time," wrote James, "but I am too far away to go home often." Like countless fathers throughout the Union and Confederate armies, he promised that when he returned, "we will have a big talk." In the meantime, "I want you to be the best little boy . . . I dont want you to Say any bad words—or cry much—I want you to be a man." Dan and Johnny later received a joint letter that assured them that "although you are little fellows I think as much of you as I do of Sam," and emphasized the importance of their helping out around the house. "I want you to play and enjoy yourselves as much as you can," wrote their father, "but you must not forget to be at home when your Mother wants you." Johnny could baby-sit their little sister while Dan could easily fetch wood, wash dishes, feed the cow, and "do a hundred little things that wont be much trouble to him, but will Save mother from getting tired."[26]

The boys frequently received congratulations from their father for their good behavior, and kind words from an approving parent never failed to follow news that they were behaving themselves at school and at home. "I have always had confidence in you," his father assured Sam, "knowing that you would do right when you reflected on your duty, and I am proud indeed to know that my confidence is well founded." To Dan, Goodnow wrote how much he appreciated the little boy's "very good letters"; "if you will only learn to write a little plainer, you will Soon do first rate." He was also immensely pleased when Nancy reported that Dan sawed and split all the wood. "I don't say go in lemons," he wrote—apparently meaning "don't let it go to your head"—"but I do say there are not many boys of your age can do that much."[27]

Few fathers were able to integrate their parenting responsibilities with their patriotic duty so thoroughly as Alva V. Cleveland of
Milwaukee, Wisconsin, who enlisted as a hospital attendant in the
Twenty-fourth Wisconsin in the fall of 1861. Accompanying him
was his twelve-year-old son George, who signed on as a drummer
boy. Although there were no doubt other father-son teams in both
armies—the drummer for the Second Minnesota in fact enlisted on
the same day and in the same company as his father, but does not
mention him again—Alva kept a diary during the pair's service. It
shows that, while both clearly sought to do their duty and rarely
complained about the army, they relished each other's companion-
ship. A number of diary entries report incidents and hardships and
dangers that most parents of underage soldiers could only fretfully
imagine; indeed, as the regiment changed trains in Chicago on their
way to Kentucky, one of George's fellow drummers fell, broke his
arm, and had to be sent home. Alva no doubt thought not only of
the family he left behind but also of his own family member in the
next railroad car when he wrote of the tearful scenes at the Kenosha
railroad station, "Such shaking of hands hugging & kissing
farewells Exchanged by Fathers & Mothers children Brothers & Sisters Friends & Neighbors it was heart rending to behold."[28]
Many parents of drummer boys would have been alarmed to
know that their sons were having the same experiences as George:
the confusion of any army on the march, the loose discipline that
characterized this green regiment, the casual supply system that
had soldiers of all age scrambling to find food wherever they could
get it, the frequent accidents that injured or killed members of the
Twenty-fourth Wisconsin, the borderline competence of the officers in the brigade (including their colonel, who was too drunk to
inspect the troops one Sunday morning), the rough sorts of men
who ended up in the army (Cleveland writes sarcastically at one
point of "our friend shaved head," who had threatened to kill the
officers). Although Cleveland's tone remains fairly objective and

even a little detached, there are hints of relief from time to time when he is able to cushion the hard life of the army for young George. The two rarely marched together (in fact, Alva normally rode in an ambulance), and George entered the "soil of old Kentuck" hours before his father, but most nights they did sleep in the same tent. When kindly ladies brought pies, cakes, jelly, and other treats to the hospital—obviously inappropriate food for sick men—Alva gave them to George. When the youngster came in from a rainy-day drill caked with mud and soaked to the skin, Alva made sure he washed his clothes and warmed himself by the fire. From time to time, especially during the chilly, muddy marches that characterized the Clevelands' wartime service, Alva was able to clear a spot in an ambulance for his son and some of the other drummers. This was particularly important during one bitterly cold march that brought Napoleon's deadly retreat from Russia to Alva's mind. He scooped George and another drummer into his ambulance, where they snuggled into blankets and the warm embrace of a friendly sergeant "in a sound slumber like the nest of pigs keeping each other warm."[29]

Occasionally Alva's duties as a father meshed perfectly with his duties as a soldier. A couple of weeks into their shared adventure, George came down with a touch of flu, "complaining of head ache with Simptoms of the camp rash." He spent a rough night in the hospital, tossing and turning and "begging me to keep that big thing from roling onto him and seeing all sorts of things." Alva bathed his head and prescribed some "downs Powder," and George eventually settled down, though he remained ill for several days. Other times Alva could just be a father. On a rare day off, the two visited an old friend, who gave them dinner and, the proud father reported, "was much pleased with George." The same day they toured a Louisville tobacco factory, bought fruit at a street market, and took in the sights. George kept his father up to date on his own adventures and accomplishments; he and the other drummers frequently went off to explore plantations and to visit Unionist ladies in nearby towns (who without fail gave them apples or candy), while one evening George announced that the drummers of the Ninth Michigan had declared him the best drummer they had seen. Reading letters from home became another father-son ritual and about a month into the diary Alva reported that they wrote a letter home, George's "first attempt at letter writing."[30]

As time went on, Alva clearly relaxed a bit, worrying less about George—or at least mentioning him less often in his diary. All that changed in mid-December 1861, when the regiment prepared for its first combat. Alva, busy readying the hospital to receive casualties, rather wistfully wrote, "I had reckoned on a march with the rest but was disappointed George had to go on without me." Alva made sure that another soldier took charge of George—and then got busy transporting his charges to a new hospital. When the regiment reached the front, however, George's captain ordered him and another drummer to stay out of harm's way, which the boys "thought . . . was hard . . . as they came to fight as well as any of them."[31]

At one point Alva mildly complained about a sleepless night in the hospital caused by too many patients and an uncomfortable cornstalk bed. But he proudly wrote that George had walked twelve miles that day and, still wearing his overcoat and shoes, went immediately to sleep. Not surprisingly, Alva "thought of home & its comforts but do not regret leaving yet, for the cause I am in is worth the sacrifice so far & I hope it will be to the end." Although George's feelings on the subject are not known, his enthusiasm for his job and his apparent uncomplaining attitude implies that he shared his father's determination and patriotism.[32]

Both Clevelands returned home safely, but not all family stories ended so well. Many fathers and many more brothers failed to return home. Their families, witnesses to the "vacant chair" of the popular wartime lament, were forever broken by the war. The letters they wrote became particularly poignant for the youngsters who grew to adulthood without fathers. Many no doubt became memorials to promises shattered by death. In 1862 a Wisconsin captain promised his three-year-old son that after the war they would build themselves a tent and "camp in it and be soldiers and [he] will see how it is." He died a year later at Vicksburg.[33]

Many children undoubtedly felt guilt over having survived when their fathers or brothers had not. A pair of Union officers unintentionally caused immeasurable psychological damage when they suggested that their well-being depended on the behavior of their children or their brothers and sisters. "When I get into Battle I might get shot," wrote one of these men, Col. Hans Heg of Wisconsin, to his daughter. "But if you are a good girl and Edmund is a good boy, God will take care of me for you." Henry Abbott of Massachusetts warned his five-year-old brother Grafton that "when you get mad & begin to cry, it makes the rebel bullets come a good deal nearer to me." Tragically, both men were killed in battle. What price did the children who received these letters pay? Were they responsible for their beloved father's or brother's death? If God chose to allow them to die, and if the children had tried their hardest to be good, did it mean that God did not care what happened to them?[34]

Such questions demonstrate the complexity of the effects of the Civil War on Northern families. Even as the separation of fathers and husbands from wives and children seems to have strengthened family bonds—the outpouring of letters fill literally thousands of published and unpublished collections of family correspondence—it inevitably threatened to destroy families through death and anguish. Much as many Civil War children seized the chance to serve their country by pitching in on the home front, family responsibilities required them to leave childhood behind prematurely.

CHAPTER FOUR

Children, Community, and the War Effort

🖋 AFTER THE FIRST DAY of fighting at Gettysburg, Tillie Pierce, who with her family had left the Rebel-occupied town to find a safe haven behind Union lines, went out to a barn where some of the injured Yankees were being cared for. "Nothing before in my experience had ever paralleled the sight we then and there beheld," she exclaimed—in words repeated by thousands of Americans who witnessed their first battles during the Civil War. "There were the groaning and crying, the struggling and dying, crowded side by side, while attendants sought to aid and relieve them as best they could." She and the friend accompanying her "were so overcome by the sad and awful spectacle that we hastened back to the house weeping bitterly." There they encountered several adult nurses making soup for the wounded. The older women tried to cheer the girls up with funny stories and good humor. "They soon dispelled our terror and caused us to laugh so much that many times when we should have been sober minded we were not; the reaction having been too sudden for our overstrung nerves." Tillie, like other Northerners who witnessed the great battle, soon grew "inured" to the bloodshed. She later looked out a window and calmly watched amputations being performed next door.[1]

Several days later Tillie toured the battlefield, climbing Little Round Top—the scene of desperate fighting on the battle's second day—to get a better view. From there she could see "the dead lying there just as they had fallen during the struggle. From the summit . . . we gazed upon the valley of death beneath. The view there spread out before us was terrible to contemplate! It was an awful spectacle! Dead soldiers, bloated horses, shattered cannon and caissons, thousands of small arms." As they walked back to town from their country refuge, they walked through fields to avoid the muddy roads. "The stench arising from the fields of carnage was most sickening. Dead horses, swollen to almost twice their natural size, lay in all directions, stains of blood frequently met our gaze, and all kinds of army accoutrements covered the ground." The landscape had been altered, "and I felt as though we were in a strange and blighted land."[2]

A different kind of blight struck the African-American residents of southeastern Pennsylvania, including the two or three hundred living in Gettysburg. As the Confederates swept into the state in the summer of 1863, patrols combed the countryside, gathering up black men, women, and children to be sent back to Virginia as slaves. Some of the prisoners were no doubt escaped slaves, but many were free blacks who had believed themselves safe. Scouring barns and fields for fleeing families, the Rebel scouts drove the people they captured—almost entirely women and children—before them, "just like we would drive cattle," wrote one white bystander. Other groups packed wagons full of captives, while young African Americans were sometimes strapped to saddles behind their captors. Whole towns were cleared of black occupants in late May and June as the slave catchers repeatedly returned to Virginia with their human plunder and then came back for more. Those who could fled by wagon, horseback, or on foot, often only at night, on back roads, or even via the old "underground railroad." White Pennsylvanians described the pitiful possessions the refugees had hurriedly scraped together and the bewildered, frightened looks on the faces of the young children and mothers who expected to be captured at any moment. One observer wrote of seeing "poor people completely worn out, carrying their families on their backs."[3]

These experiences were highly unusual for Northern children. Although disruption was not nearly as intense in the North as in the Confederacy, many aspects of the communities in which Yankee children lived were touched by the Civil War. A study of the home front in Maryland illustrates a few of the conditions and events affecting communities in general and children in particular that occurred elsewhere in the North. In Maryland a number of schools were forced to close their doors. Some suffered from the dramatic fall in enrollment caused by the withdrawal of students from the Southern states; others, located in the path of invading Confederate armies in 1862 and 1863, suffered material losses that doomed them to closure; still others, like several in Annapolis, lost students when parents refused to let them attend schools located so close to the presence of "immoral" and disease-ridden soldiers. Public schools also suffered as the economic downturn early in the war forced parents to take their children out of school and put them to work (public schools in the 1860s usually required parents to pay tuition). Conversely, the economic boom that began in 1863 encouraged many male students to seek well-paying jobs in industries that normally would have been filled by the able-bodied men now serving in the army. Enrollment at Central High School in Baltimore fell by 20 percent, to only 205, during the 1864–1865 school year.[4]

Tillie's descriptions of the ravaged countryside and of the human cost of the Civil War were unusual for a Northern memoirist. Since most of the fighting took place within the Confederacy, very few Yankee children actually saw war firsthand. As a result, while invasion and destruction were integral parts of the war for Southern children and the communities in which they lived, Northern communities experienced war very differently. Still, like their

Southern counterparts, Northern children and youth inserted themselves enthusiastically into war activities and issues, taking their
places as members of the larger communities in which they lived.

We Live in Historic Times

To hear ten-year-old Hermon DeLong tell it, the little upstate New
York town of Dansville provided an idyllic childhood. His father
worked hard but made a comfortable living; there were plenty of
boys with whom he could play baseball and ramble through the surrounding countryside; even his school days created cherished memories late in his life. "And then," as Abraham Lincoln would later
declare enigmatically in his second inaugural address, "the war
came." Hermon wrote many years later that the war drew in everything and everyone, including children. "One need not be a grown-
up to imbibe the peculiar feeling that hangs over everything in time
of war." He compared it to the "sensation that goes about when a
contagious disease suddenly breaks out in a peaceful community
and the infected houses are placarded and streets barricaded." Unfortunately, no quarantine could keep the disease of war out, even
in a safe little town like his: "Young and old felt it weighing down
like an incubus, and when . . . we heard the news that Sumter had
been fired upon and the blank walls were covered with calls for volunteers, our happy town seemed suddenly to grow grim and forbid-
ding." But the town, despite its distance from the "seat of strife . . .
stepped into the arena and picked up her sword as defiantly as
though the boom of battle were echoing from her protecting hills."[5]

The pride with which Hermon recalled his hometown's patriotism carried over to his memories of how he and his friends reacted
to the crisis: "We ten-year-olds felt the shock keenly but met it
bravely." This sums up the responses of most Northern children to
the challenges faced by their communities. They eagerly joined the

political and military hoopla that accompanied the beginning of the war, which one boy later called "a thrilling as well as a sad time." They contributed to the massive home-front campaign to raise money for soldiers' causes, and, as soldiers' orphans, became symbols of the nation's sacrifice and recipients of its patriotic benevolence. They were integrated fully into their world at war, and would not have wanted it any other way.[6]

Children's magazines sought to make sure that children understood they had a role to play in the war. A tradition in most publications for children before the war had been a section devoted to correspondence, games, and discussions, with a conversational, even homey tone for its readers. Oliver Optic called his column for the *Student and Schoolmate* the "Teacher's Desk," while *Forrester's Playmate* published a "Chat with Readers and Correspondents" each month, illustrated by a family gathering in a cozy parlor, complete with napping dog.

Optic devoted many of his columns to information and opinions about the war. He frequently highlighted the notion of sacrifice and assured readers that, first of all, they were a part of the war effort and might be required to make sacrifices, and second, that they were not alone in their loss and hardship. During the winter of 1862–1863, as the North reeled from the military disaster at Fredericksburg and the recently issued Emancipation Proclamation caused a firestorm of debate over the racial future of the United States, Optic compared the dark days of the present to another time of crisis. "Never since the days of the Revolution, have the courage and fortitude of the American people been so severely tried as at the present time. . . . Defeat and disaster follow defeat and disaster so rapidly, that we are not permitted to recover from the effects of one, before we are confronted by another." Yet, he claimed, the country had not sunken into "general despondency." The people retained their faith in the principles for which they began the fight and were confident that their flag still represented freedom. "We have often reminded our young readers of the fact that they live in historic times; in a period whose every day will be a page for future ages to read." Children must appreciate the gravity of these years and take the appropriate messages from the events they witnessed. Drawing again on the Revolutionary rhetoric that inspired both the North and the South, Optic declared that "the days that try men's souls are upon us—may we be equal to the occasion!" Even though most Northerners—except for those who had lost loved ones—had not had to suffer much so far, "we may be called upon to endure more, to make great sacrifices of comfort and plenty; if we are, let us show our devotion to the great cause by suffering without a murmur." The best way for children to contribute to their communities, to be a part of the great cause for which their fathers and brothers and neighbors were fighting, was to be "true to God, true to ourselves, [and] true to the historic character our fathers bequeathed to us."[7]

Not quite a year later, months after the great victories at Gettysburg and Vicksburg had failed to end the rebellion, *Forrester's Playmate* invited its readers to sit down and chat: "Come in, friends, and carefully close the door. There is a cheerful fire to greet you here, and your accustomed place at our circle awaits you." The beginning of a new year brought thoughts of earlier failures but also of fresh starts, as well as memories of losses and regrets. The column for January 1864 never mentions the war as such, but it is not hard to fit the conflict into its message of optimism tinged with sadness and its effort to comfort readers who had endured the death of a friend or loved one in 1863. "How sad it seemed to part with them, and to see their bodies committed to the cold ground." But everyone should be comforted—in times of war as well as peace, the author implies—that "they have simply *gone a little way before us*. We shall as surely overtake them as time moves onward." This simple faith in happy reunions in a blissful hereafter was a way of uniting all children of war, a way to assure youngsters afraid for the future and for their own lives and the lives of the people they loved. "And so I trust that every reader of the Playmate will go into the new year, with gratitude for past blessings, good resolutions for the future, and a mind at peace with all men."[8]

Pious assurances may have comforted youngsters in times of despair, but it was the excitement of war preparations and politics that fascinated them most. Children felt themselves drawn into the larger community through the emotional glue provided by political and military events and rallies. Just as they had before 1861, Civil War children eagerly inserted themselves with their fathers and older brothers into the emotional political battles of wartime, especially the colorful demonstrations and parades. During the presidential campaign in 1864, seven-year-old Henrietta Dana and her father Richard—one of the founders of the Republican party in Massachusetts—left the dinner table and dashed outside when they heard the drum-and-fife music that was an inevitable feature of any political procession. They raced through the narrow Boston streets and "struck, in full blast of cheering and enthusiasm, a *Democratic* torchlight procession!" Despite their ardent Republicanism, "when the band piped up the exhilarating strains of 'Roy's Wife of Aldivallach,' politics were thrown to the winds," and the pair "tramped the maze of Boston's down-town streets," Henrietta bouncing on her father's shoulders, for half an hour. When father and daughter finally returned home, they were "jeered at by our good Republican household" and had to eat a cold supper. Redemption arrived later in the campaign when they attended a Republican parade. Watching from a second-story window, the "moving masses of men and boys in their long dominos and hoods, with the flaring torches, the gay colored lanterns, floats, and illuminated transparencies with their mottoes and slogans, the blare of brass bands, the crowds cheering and whistling, or shouting the choruses of popular war-songs, it was a picture to remain long in a child's memory."[9]

Yet the political situation, at least as Henrietta remembered it fifty years later, was more unsettled than it appeared. Lincoln was not popular among the circles in which her father operated; "he was a Western rural politician, whose election seemed to many a national calamity." As an adult, Henrietta was rather apologetic: "I am afraid we children saw him only through the distressed and doubtful eyes of our elders." In their play, when they acted out scenes from the great national crisis, "I cannot remember any of us, boy or girl, choosing the part of Lincoln."[10]

A similar ambiguity characterized the response to wartime politics of James Sullivan, a Carlisle, Pennsylvania, teenager who had cut his political eyeteeth on the political crises of the 1850s. A Democrat since he could remember, he was a great admirer of Gen. George B. McClellan, under whose command his older brother Tom had served. Tom died at the Battle of South Mountain in 1862; in his last letter to James he had reiterated his support for "Little Mac," who had just been reinstated to his command of the Army of the Potomac. Two years later James was stunned and hurt when he learned that the same Democrats who had nominated McClellan for president had also declared that the war was a failure. "That reckless utterance of political extremists completely threw me off my mental balance." He wanted to follow "his party," but his brother had died fighting for the Union, and that Union must be maintained by continuing the war. "I was for McClellan, but I was also for the war." If the war was a failure, Tom had died for nothing. The dilemma thrust this boy who would not be allowed to vote for another six or seven years into "a fever of uncertainty as to my political duty."[11]

Even in a safe little town in upstate New York, Hermon DeLong remembered, boys reveled in the recruiting drives, the sight of "awkward squads drilling on the public square," the departure of troops for the front, and war rallies. They sang sentimental war songs like "Tenting Tonight," "Dear Mother, I've Come Home to Die," and "The Vacant Chair" while picking lint and sewing bandages for the U.S. Sanitary Commission, the organization that coordinated home-front efforts to raise money and gather supplies for the army. They practiced politics, with the community of boys "about equally divided between . . . Black Abolitionists and Copperheads," each side choosing familiar symbols: young Copperheads boasted Indian-head pins sliced out of copper pennies, while Republicans fitted themselves out with the traditional Republican "wide-awake" gear of "caps, capes, and torches." Boys had a public role to play too; when war bulletins arrived at the telegraph office, they would read them to the assembled crowd. And they became part of the shared sacrifice of wartime, especially when the mother of a local soldier killed in battle invited a group of boys to view the body. "In the midst of her grief there was a strong Spartan pride in the sacrifice she had made and she knew the lesson to us young Americans would be a good one."[12]

The chance to be part of the war effort captivated many Northern children, who made "housewives" (small leather folders containing sewing supplies) for the soldiers, contributed books to soldiers' hospitals, and gathered food and bedding to be put into huge boxes sent to the front. Sunday School students banded together to buy religious tracts for soldiers while schools took on the responsibility for raising money and sending supplies to specific regiments and hospitals. In a rare newspaper article devoted to blacks' contributions to the war effort, the Philadelphia *Christian Recorder* reported that the Bethel African Methodist Episcopal Sabbath School had raised money for both the local Soldiers' Aid Society and for a hospital organized for a regiment of black soldiers. The *New York Times* encouraged children to plant onions to be sent to the army, while organizations with names like the Alert Club and the Bird's Nest Bank raised money for soldiers' causes by collecting pennies. Some children contributed money and supplies to organizations aiding the freedmen in the South and Unionist refugees from East Tennessee.[13]

A girl who went with her mother to Soldiers' Aid Society meetings at her local Baptist church was pulled into the patriotic orbit of

SIX AND EIGHTY-SIX KNITTING FOR THE SOLDIERS.

Children and adults alike devoted spare moments to easing the plight of Union soldiers. *(Frank B. Goodrich, The Tribute Book, 1865)*

the community of women who met each week to make bandages, sew, and pack food and supplies into boxes. The little girls made lint that would be used to bandage wounds. As they and their mothers and older sisters worked, someone would often read letters from relatives or beaus "describing camp scenes, or battle experiences, or hair-breadth escapes from Libby Prison." The ambience of patriotic philanthropy "thrilled us and left indelible memories," she remembered years later. "Very important we children felt as we scraped away at the linen, making fluffy piles of the soft lint."[14]

Although their older sisters may have sensed it, little girls like this one could not have known of the sometimes furious debate over the appropriate roles of women during the war. One of the battlefields for this struggle was the Sanitary Commission, where the male-dominated leadership of the national office tended to downplay women's practical contributions, despite the dynamic leadership and hard work of such patriots as Mary Ann Bickerdyke, who worked tirelessly to bring supplies to armies in the Western theater, and the better-known Clara Barton, who concentrated her efforts on improving medical care for the Army of the Potomac in the east. Women frequently saw their work, which often took them out of their homes, introduced them to assembly-line production techniques, and made them part of organizations that extended beyond their traditional circles of church and community, as a powerful agent of change in their lives. Men cared more for the knitting and cooking and nurturing performed by women, and continued to think of them as secondary contributors and sentimental patriots.

Not everyone appreciated the dreary, tedious patriotism of lint-picking. As if he understood the larger argument over the proper kind of war work for women, Maurice Egan remembered that he and his nine-year-old friends, unable to become drummer boys, "were reduced to making lint for the army"—with the girls. When one little girl expressed her confusion over why exactly they were picking lint, her older brother stunned her by grabbing her arm, pricking it with a pin, and then packing the lint around the tiny wound. "I squealed of course: he looked at me very gravely and said, 'Alice, the soldiers never cry.'"[15]

Of course it was easier to feel part of the cause, to feel at the center of the adult world clashing around them, if one lived in Washington, D.C. Despite its grime and mud and the seeming impermanence of most of its buildings, Washington was still the fulcrum of the Union war effort and an exciting place for a child to live during the war. "We lived years in as many days," Elizabeth Vincent recalled sixty years later, "and we grew old suddenly." The latest information from the front was a valuable commodity, and "the cry of the newsboy was the signal for windows to go up at night—any time of night—in response to his call." Political news and gossip came from a clerk who lived in their spare room; Eliza-

THE OLD WOMAN WHO LIVED IN A SHOE

One of the most popular booths at Sanitary Fairs featured girls dressed as the hapless nursery-rhyme mother with "so many children she didn't know what to do." *(Frank B. Goodrich, The Tribute Book, 1865)*

beth frequently saw Lincoln going to and from church—and shook his hand (twice!) at a White House reception; the *USS Monitor* could be viewed at the Navy Yard; and, of course, soldiers, some wearing fantastic Zouave uniforms, filled the streets. Elizabeth visited the hospitals that sprang up on the outskirts of town, and when Lincoln was assassinated she was among the throngs who stood in line for hours to see his body lying in state.[16]

All these activities invited children to act as members of the communities in which they lived. But the most massive community-wide efforts involving children were the giant fairs staged by the Sanitary Commission to raise money for their efforts to purchase medical supplies, create military hospitals, hire doctors and nurses, deliver mail, and provide rest homes near railroad depots for soldiers going to and returning from the army.

It took a great deal of money to finance these programs, which the Sanitary Commission raised through "Sanitary Fairs" sponsored by towns and cities throughout the North. The fairs displayed community involvement at its finest and included the contributions of individual children as well as members of schools, orphanages, Sunday Schools, and other groups. Symbolic of these efforts were the young girls who worked four-hour shifts dressed as the Old Woman Who Lived in a Shoe, perched in a giant shoe and surrounded by their children—dolls that were for sale. The most famous was Nellie Grant, who played the role at the St. Louis Sanitary Fair in 1864. Nellie's mother, Julia Dent Grant, wrote that the nine-year-old "was delighted with her metamorphosis" into the nursery-rhyme character, "seated as she was in a mammoth black pasteboard shoe filled with beautiful dolls of all sizes," costumed in "a ruffled cap and a pair of huge spectacles." Each doll she sold earned the fair fifty cents, as did prints of a photograph of Nellie in full costume.[17]

At New York's 1864 fair, a separate Children's Department occupied the entire east wing of the Union Square Building. There visitors to the fair found booths and displays sponsored and staffed by public and private schools, a toy store, and soldiers' orphans. According to the fair newspaper, the items made and sold by the city's youngsters "represent probably a greater devotion than in almost any other department." For instance, "the little children of the Home for the Friendless" gave hundreds of pennies and made "lamplighters" out of colored paper. The article highlighted a poignant source of inspiration for these children: more than sixty former inmates of the Home were in the army. Other institutions donating handmade items included the Deaf and Dumb Asylum, the Blind Asylum, the Wilson Industrial School, the Birch Church Mission School, the "girls of the House of Refuge," members of the Hebrew Orphan Asylum, unidentified "blind girls," and the "Children of the Sacred Heart" in Harlem. African-American children appear here and there on lists of participants. In Brooklyn, youngsters from the "Colored Home" made an unspecified contribution to the fair. [18]

A story that came out of the Great Central Fair in Philadelphia became something of a Sanitary Fair legend, replicated at least anecdotally in a number of cities. In Philadelphia, the story went, a ten-year-old boy had nothing to give to the fair but his pet dog. Learning of his sacrifice, the chairwoman of the Department of Singing Birds and Pet Animals bought the little terrier and returned it to its grateful owner. Other versions featured kittens rather than dogs, but the message remained the same: if a child could give up its most precious possession on behalf of the soldiers, adults needed to dig deep too.[19]

Sanitary Fairs mustered thousands of children as participants and as consumers, and schools put together massive mobilization efforts in support of the fairs. Perhaps forty public and private schools in New York raised $24,000 by holding reading lessons and entertainments for their families and friends during the Metropolitan Fair. Philadelphia's schoolchildren were even more active. For months before the fair, 1,400 teachers and 72,000 pupils made handicrafts, rehearsed concerts, readings, and tableaux, and held tea parties and festivals to raise money for the Great Central Fair. Cincinatti schoolchildren conducted "gymnastic exercises" and other entertainments at the Great Western Fair. In St. Louis, 1,700 students from the city's many German schools sang during the ceremonial procession and recession while Nellie Grant read fairy tales to throngs of children. A single performance of "Cinderella," featuring 200 child dancers and John C. and Jessie Benton Fremont's son as the prince, earned $2,500 in New York City.[20]

Chicago hosted two of the biggest Sanitary Fairs of the war, and young Chicagoans kicked into high gear to support the Northwestern Branch of the Sanitary Commission. At the opening ceremonies of the first fair, held in the late summer of 1863, three hundred "young misses" sang "The Great Rebellion," a "patriotic musical allegory." At one of several private entertainments, an Evanston doctor's children raised ten dollars with a "tableaux party." Rock Island schoolchildren collected pickled tomatoes and vowed to contribute a nickel a month until the end of the war.[21]

In addition to these mass efforts, children contributed individually. Many held their own fairs in backyards, front porches, or parlors. A reporter for the *Chicago Tribune* visited one of these "interesting and patriotic fairs of the little ones." He described the "flags, banners, emblems, and pictures" that decorated the yard; marveled at tables groaning with "choice" fruits, cream lemonade, and cake; and admired the "veritable fairy queens" who had organized the event and charmed "the quarters and dimes out of the purses of the visitors in an unaccountable manner." *The Tribute Book* applauded the work of ten ten-year-old Brooklyn girls who each held their own backyard fair and brought in an average of $16.50: "There are doubtless ten millionaires in the land who have not done as much in proportion." Young Willie Kingsbury raised money by selling handmade items to neighborhood children as well as kisses from a "pretty little fair-haired boy" who lived nearby. He also donated the pennies he earned for finding sewing pins— a penny for every pin he found. His enthusiasm was rewarded with a trip to the Sanitary Fair in New York.[22]

New York also saw the most extreme example of the dark underside of youngsters' efforts to fit into their communities—and of one of the most painful ways in which Northern children became victims of the Civil War. Americans throughout the North resisted military conscription when it was instituted in the summer of 1863, but the worst violence broke out in the Union's largest city. Beginning July 13, mostly working-class New Yorkers rioted for five days, causing millions of dollars in damage and the deaths of at least one hundred people before police and army units ended the carnage. Rampaging through the poorest sections of the city as well as some of the more affluent neighborhoods, mobs targeted military sites,

Many children raised money for the Sanitary Commission by holding fairs in backyards or on front steps. *(Frank B. Goodrich, The Tribute Book, 1865)*

transportation facilities, and the homes and businesses of Republican leaders. But, reflecting their disgust at the federal government's adoption of the emancipation of the slaves as a war aim, they also took out their anger on African Americans, burning their homes and beating up and lynching a number of men. Young boys and teenagers took part in the violence; youngsters would "mark" the houses of African Americans by throwing rocks through windows, then lead older boys and men back to drive the residents out. Others joined men in the almost ritualistic torture, mutilation, and killing of a number of black men. Patrick Butler, a sixteen-year-old mentioned in contemporary accounts of the rioting, gained notoriety when he helped lynch a crippled coachman, then earned rounds of applause from the mob when he dragged the man's body through the streets by the genitals.[23]

African-American children were also attacked by the rioters. A number of boys and girls were assaulted while hundreds of children were among the refugees who scattered, leaving most of their paltry belongings behind, to communities on Long Island and New Jersey. At least two died: a black baby was thrown from a window by a mob, and Joseph Reed, a seven-year-old, was beaten to death. A report issued shortly after the riot highlighted Joseph's religious fervor; his pastor referred to him as the "child martyr." The most spectacular attack on black children occurred on the riot's first day, when a mob sacked and burned the four-story Colored Orphans' Asylum on Fifth Avenue and Forty-second Street. Home to well over two hundred orphans and, according to one historian, "an imposing symbol of white charity toward blacks and black upward mobility," the Asylum also became a focus of racial hatred. Thousands of men, women, and children descended on it late in the afternoon of July 13, dragging most of the furniture and supplies out of the building before setting it on fire. Incredibly, the children, led by the white superintendent and matron, escaped from the besieged building unharmed. They found refuge at a police station several blocks away.[24]

United We Stand, Divided We Fall

Besides taking part in activities organized by adults, children also joined the larger community in expressing their views on the rebellion and on its related political issues. A number of youngsters, especially in New England, issued their own newspapers. Some

An engraving of the pillaging and destruction of New York's Colored Orphans' Asylum during the draft riots of July 1863. *(Illustrated London News, August 15, 1863)*

were professionally printed while others were written by hand; some had runs of a year or two, others of only a few issues; a few apparently had circulations of a hundred or more while others were read only by family members and friends. But the editors of all of them sought to be part of the community of Northern citizens mobilized to help the government put down the rebellion. They tended to be hybrids of traditional newspapers and juvenile magazines, with the same combination of serious articles, humorous pieces, sentimental poetry, and human interest stories. Yet the editors of these juvenile newspapers—called "amateur" newspapers later in the century—replicated the great political and social debates of the day, using the arguments and styles of "adult" newspapers as well as juvenile magazines.

The amateur publishers of these newspapers described the spirit of shared sacrifice that characterized the Northern war effort. The editor of the Providence *Sunbeam* acknowledged that while he and his siblings were "comfortable and happy," thousands of children had been "deprived of friends and homes, by this cruel war. We do not forget them, but often wish we could do something for their comfort." The New Year's editorial for 1864 gratefully reported that "Health, and happiness have been bestowed upon us: the lives of our friends have been spared, and each day has seemed to bring some new source of comfort and enjoyment." But "How different the lot of many about us. This cruel war has brought sorrow and sadness into many homes. Fathers and brothers have been taken, and many children, who, at the commencement of the last year, were as happy as we, are now left orphans." Sometimes, however, the war hit close to home. Another edition included a loving obituary of a young relative who had died of disease in the army. He had been "a good son, a kind brother, a faithful friend, and a brave officer. His end was peaceful, for his hope was in Jesus."[25]

Other pieces provided the kind of trivia and filler common to newspapers and children's periodicals alike. Writers described visits to nearby military installations and encampments, glimpses of famous generals and politicians, the comings and goings of local regiments, and little tidbits like the supposed fact that at least a hundred Rebel officers had each lost a leg during the first three years of the war. *Once a Fortnight* offered a column filled with short news stories from the front, from troop movements and changes of command to reports of skirmishes and sea raiders. Most newspapers around the country printed letters from soldiers, and some amateur editors did the same. The *Sunbeam* featured a letter from a chaplain in the Third Rhode Island Heavy Artillery, who described camp life as well as the "strange scenes I have witnessed . . . and what strange experiences have been my portion, among towns, cities, plains, mountains, vallies [sic], islands; in battles with cavalry, infantry, artillery, guerillas, and pirates; and how often have I known the terrible trials of bloody fields." Another paper published in Providence, the *Rhode Island Sun*, also included a section called "From the War," with brief notes written by a friend serving in the Union army during the Peninsula campaign in the summer of 1862. The correspondent mostly made fun of the African Americans he encountered and complained about the mosquitoes.[26]

The language used by many of the editors indicates that they considered themselves members of the body politic—despite the unfortunate fact that they were too young to vote or to serve in the army. Words like "our" and "we" appeared regularly in war-related articles in the Pawtucket *Union*, which in April 1862 reported that, "Notwithstanding we have had so many traitors to contend with, there have been a great many victories won by our Generals and our heroic Burnside. . . . May he continue until every rebel is crushed out and the Stars and Stripes wave over the Capitol of every State where disunion now reigns." The *Sunbeam* argued that, though "war is, in itself, an evil of great magnitude," if the Union won, "Our government will thereby gain a reputation for power which will extend to all the nations of the globe. People from other lands will seek refuge under our flag, and be willing to join with us in the support of such a government as ours. . . . Who would not prefer living in such a land, rather than where the Government is at any time liable to be overthrown and destroyed."[27]

Perhaps no group of editors supported the war effort, promoted the reelection of Abraham Lincoln, and opposed slavery more strenuously than the youngsters who published the amateur newspapers of New England. *Once a Fortnight*, published in Worcester, followed the lead of adult newspapers when it ran a masthead that included "For President—Abraham Lincoln. For Vice-President—Andrew Johnson." The most forthrightly abolitionist paper was the *Sunbeam*, which declared, "How wonderful is this war in its origin: Slavery stabbing Freedom! How wonderful in its results: Slavery prostrate, and gasping in its grave!"[28]

During the dark days of the late summer of 1864, when Union armies were stalemated in Georgia and before Petersburg, and casualties mounted to unprecedented levels, the Concord *Observor* printed editorial after editorial beseeching Northerners to press the fight. "Although disasters and defeats may crown our efforts," the editor admitted in August 1864, "remember that the only key to our future prosperity and fame rests upon victory alone; and victory is dependent upon the people. Let every loyal and true born American suppose that unless he threw in his mite towards crushing this awful and devastating rebellion, we shall be conquered and forever kept beneath the foot of Slavery and Oppression. War must become the daily vocation of us all." Two weeks later he lamented the "fact that there is a stronger and more influential army of conspiring traitors and rebel sympathizers at our backs than we have to battle on the fields before us," so many in Massachusetts, in fact, that some newspapers were promoting the Copperhead cause. "Shameful! Shameful!" he thundered. Later in the fall, just before the election, the *Observor* made one last plea for voters to reelect Lincoln: "Let every man, with a solemn renewal of his Union vows be prepared to give in an overwhelming majority for Lincoln and Johnson, the prosecution of the war, and the final extermination of slavery."[29]

The most complete public response of Northern youth to the Civil War appeared in a handwritten monthly newspaper called *The Athenaeum*, published by the boys at Newark (New Jersey) High School during the last two years of the war. Most of the pieces apparently originated as class assignments, submitted by their authors to the boy editors, who sometimes complained because they were not receiving enough essays from their classmates. Many of the essays, poems, and illustrations (normally one very detailed line drawing for each issue) were on typical Victorian subjects as natural

The title page for *The Athenaeum,* published by the boys at Newark
High School. *(New Jersey Historical Society)*

philosophy, ethics, and family duties. An article on "Perfection" suggested that everyone should strive to do their best; "What a Contrast" offered vignettes contrasting urban and rural areas, rich and poor, hot and cold weather; "The First Baby" reflected on the joys of starting a family; "Winter Coming" poetically welcomed the onset of cold weather.

But as members of the larger community, the editors were particularly interested in joining the national debate over the issues that had brought on the war, and the effect of the war on Northern society. *The Athenaeum's* motto was "United We Stand, Divided We Fall," and the editors presented a coherent pro-Union, pro-Republican, and anti-slavery platform. An illustration appearing in the May 1864 edition showed a Union cavalryman plunging his sword through the breast of a Confederate over the caption "A Blow for the Flag." The cover sheet for the second volume retained the original motto but also included a picture of the Goddess of Liberty placing a garland wreath on the head of a small African-American child. Although most of the articles dealt with national events, one described the homecoming of the Eighth New Jersey in the fall of 1864, a regiment that had participated in most of the major battles fought by the Army of the Potomac and that had returned home with "very few of its original members nearly all of them having been killed in battle."[30]

War-related articles ranged from a two-part narrative of a classmate's hair-raising escape from the 1863 sack of Lawrence, Kansas, to an editorial arguing that the moral courage of patriots had to match their physical courage. One curious piece traced the "career" of a leather boot, from the slaughterhouse and tannery through bloody military campaigns, Libby Prison, and a dramatic escape, to its final resting place as a war "memento" in its wearer's closet. Verse was not the strongest feature of *The Athenaeum*, but occasionally an intrepid poet explored some element of the war. Typical in its sentiments—and its quality—was a poem saluting the hero of Vicksburg, "General Grant." Its third verse read:

> When treasons [sic] barrier would prevail
> When traitors in the dust would trail
> Union banner of Liberty
> His dauntless arm he interposed
> And rebellious plots disclosed
> Unfurling the flag of the free.[31]

Not every *Athenaeum* article took the war seriously. The New Jersey state election of 1863 was described in a mock biblical tone: "Now it came to pass in the third year of the reign of Abraham the president; in the eleventh month on the third day of the month, that all the people on the north of the line, even the great line of Mason & Dixie, gathered themselves together, every man to his place, to elect men who should go in and out before them, and who should speak for them. . . ." In "Uncle Zeke at the Fair," an old man battles crowds and high prices at the local Sanitary Fair. Disappointed in his failure to negotiate a smaller admission fee, he forgoes the armory department (housing captured weapons and other equipment) when he finds out he has to pay extra to get in. He does buy some calico, an expensive glass of soda water, and a "dancing nigger"—apparently a toy—for his nephew.[32]

Like editors of the great metropolitan dailies, the boys who guided *The Athenaeum* provided a New Year's summary of the events of 1863, "The Old and New Year." They traced events from the issuing of the Emancipation Proclamation on January 1 through the great victories at Gettysburg, Vicksburg, and Chattanooga. At times during the year, "the very existence of the nation seemed trembling in the balance," but eventually Union arms prevailed and the year ended on a high note. "But these victories," the editors reminded their readers, "have not been secured without great loss of life, and while we rejoice over our victories, let us not forget the many houses that have been made desolate during the past year by the ravages of war." Like many an adult newspaperman's New Year's editorial in 1864, this one ended with the hope that "if it be the will of Providence may it be a happy year to our beloved land. And may the close of this year witness the close of the struggle and the return of unity and peace to our now divided and distracted country." Another article in the same issue shared another characteristic of the newspapers produced by and for adults: premature optimism. "Appearances are now that very soon the banner we love, will not have one opposing enemy," predicted the editors. "The leading men of the rebel armies are getting discouraged and the privates of their armies are almost persuaded to lay down their arms." The war would go on for fifteen bloody months.[33]

Finally, although they did not offer many articles on the subject, the editors clearly approved of the decision to make the eradication of slavery a war aim of the United States. An article called simply "Slavery" began with "What a long catalogue of crime and blood-shed on the one side and of helpless suffering on the other, is comprised in this single word." Slavery violated both the Declaration of Independence and the Golden Rule. Like many public speeches and pamphlets of the day, the article forged a narrative of slavery's long history dating back to the origins of the European slave trade in the early sixteenth century. The author goes on to dismiss at least two of the traditional justifications of slavery—that whites were not capable of performing such hard labor, and that the Bible supported the institution as it existed in the South. And like most white males in the North, the editorialist denies he is seeking equality for African Americans: "We do not say that they should mix in and associate with us as we would with those of our own family or nation, but we do say that they should be left free to act for themselves."[34]

A typical illustration from *The Athenaeum*—this one is captioned "A Blow for the Flag." *(New Jersey Historical Society)*

My Father Loved Me Dearly

As Governor Andrew Curtin of Pennsylvania prepared to celebrate the first official Thanksgiving in November 1863, he was interrupted by a knock at the door of his Harrisburg mansion. Upon answering, he discovered two little children begging for food. They said they were orphans whose father had been killed in the war. Instantly, Curtin later remembered, he realized that something had to be done about the nation's war orphans. "Great God!" he recalled himself exclaiming, "is it possible that the people of Pennsylvania can feast this day while the children of her soldiers who have fallen in the war beg bread from door to door?"[35]

Although the incident may be apocryphal, it certainly made for heart-wrenching mythology. Children's magazines had frequently featured soldiers' orphans in tearjerkers like the poem "The Soldier's Little Daughter," in which the kindly narrator encounters a seven-year-old beggar whose mother has died and whose father is away at war. The narrator buys her bread and takes her to his lonely garret, where the girl tells him,

> "My name is Nellie Grover, sir;
> My father loved me dearly;
> And is it true as people say,
> That the war is ended, nearly?"

> 'Twas strange, but as she spoke, I chanced
> To look my paper over;
> And there I read,—"*shot through the heart,*
> *A private, William Grover.*"

The narrator vows on the spot to care for the little girl.[36]

Such ad hoc and personal solutions for the major social welfare issues raised by the Civil War were not enough, and many states responded with programs aimed at caring for the families of absent soldiers and, later, for soldiers' orphans. Much of the aid extended to soldiers' families came informally from churches, town and village governments, and other charitable organizations. But the magnitude of the need outstripped the ability of these institutions to distribute aid in traditional ways. The experience of Cincinnati, a bustling city of more than 160,000, shows the varying methods and multiple forms of relief provided by most Northern communities.

As early as 1862 the Cincinnati Relief Union—a privately funded organization founded before the war to prevent street begging, find jobs for the needy, and, in some cases, hand out food, clothing, and fuel (but never cash) to the indigent—found its case-load dominated by soldiers' families. By January 1865, of the 2,000 families on the Union's books, about 1,500 belonged to soldiers. In addition, military committees organized at the ward level for the purpose of recruiting soldiers and raising money for the bounties offered by local authorities to volunteers also distributed relief to those volunteers' families. One ward raised money by holding an oyster supper at which well-known politicians and Gen. William S. Rosecrans gave speeches. During the fair held by the Sanitary Commission in Cincinnati in 1864, the $7,500 in proceeds from a special ball and a dinner were donated to local families. As the size of the war effort grew, as more men went to the army, and as other factors intervened, such as the inability of army paymasters to keep up with the many Ohio soldiers marching through Georgia and the Carolinas with Gen. William T. Sherman, state and local officials increased their efforts. The governor of Ohio asked farmers to bring firewood and food contributions into the towns, a massive fundraising campaign called the "Testimonial to Soldiers' Families" was launched, and late in 1864 a "Grand Donation Supper" was held at the Burnet House in Cincinnati. Although reliable figures are not available, in Cincinnati the number of soldiers' families requiring relief probably reached a high of four thousand in November 1864; statewide, at the end of the war, more than 44,000 families of soldiers were deemed "necessitous" of aid.[37]

Communities also extended aid to hard-pressed black families. In St. Louis, as in other areas of the Union where slavery existed, special organizations appeared to care for black refugees and other victims of war. The Western Sanitary Commission, the Freedmen's Relief Society, and the Ladies Union Aid Society helped with food, clothing, shelter, and medical care while the American Missionary Association, as it did throughout the occupied parts of the Confederacy, established schools for black children and adults. In just a few months the Committee of Merchants for the Relief of Colored

People raised over $40,000 and collected more than two thousand articles of clothing for the hundreds of African Americans left homeless by the draft riots. Soldiers' families often received special treatment from local governments. Wives and children of recruits—including black soldiers, who for many months were paid less than their white counterparts—received small cash payments, coal or wood for cooking and heating, and sometimes food.[38]

Into this mix of public and private philanthropy stepped Pennsylvania's Governor Curtin, who followed up his Thanksgiving Day inspiration by obtaining a $50,000 grant from the Pennsylvania Railroad to establish soldiers' orphans' schools. Eventually more than fifteen separate schools contracted with the state to provide homes and education for Pennsylvania's war orphans.[39]

But Curtin was not the only Northern politician concerned with the children of killed and maimed soldiers. In his second inaugural address, President Lincoln had promised to care for "him who have borne the battles, and for his widow, and his orphan." Late in the war Congress passed a two-dollars-per-month pension for the children of deceased soldiers, but most programs for soldiers' orphans were developed at the local and state levels. The Institute of Reward for Orphans of Patriots began raising money for scholarships and other educational programs in 1862 while New Yorkers established the New York State Volunteer Institute, a military school for male orphans, the Union Home School for the Children of Volunteers, and the Patriot Orphan Home. A temporary school for the children of Iowa orphans opened in 1864, funded at least partly by donations from Iowa soldiers.[40]

The massive casualties of the war clearly put pressure on institutions for fatherless children. The number of boys seeking shelter in New York Newsboys Lodging House nearly doubled; the Northern Home for Friendless Children reported that half of its 160 residents were the children of soldiers; and well over a fourth of the 575 children admitted into Milwaukee asylums were related to soldiers. With existing facilities bursting at the seams, philanthropists and religious denominations throughout the North scrambled to establish new institutions for the children of soldiers. So great was the demand that Methodists in Boston, Baptists in Louisville, Jews in Cleveland, members of the Reformed Church in Philadelphia, and Roman Catholics in a number of cities opened new homes for orphans. Mainly due to the absence or loss of fathers at war, as many orphanages opened in the 1860s as in the two preceding decades combined.

In some cases, orphanages loosened their regulations to adjust to the exigencies of war. The Chicago Orphan Asylum added a clause to its bylaws early in the war to admit "Children of soldiers who are in the army or who have been in the service of the United States, and whose children are in destitute circumstances." The Catholic Home for Destitute Children designed a special category of "Civil War Wards." The influx of the children of Civil War soldiers did not always go well; the historian of the Cincinnati Orphan Asylum, whose 126 residents in 1866 included 100 children of soldiers (supported in part by donations from the Sanitary Commission), blamed the unrest that plagued the institution during and just after the war on "the wild, untamable offspring of Civil War veterans." The trustees even considered turning away soldiers' children to preserve the peace.[41]

The pressure on orphanages and other institutions for children continued after the war, when most Northern states established soldiers' orphans' homes, and when those young survivors of the saviors of the Union became potent symbols of sacrifice and patriotism.

Northern children had always felt a part of the communities in which they lived. They had been nonvoting but vocal participants in political campaigns and shrewd observers of current events. The war amplified their experiences, providing many opportunities for joining parents and other adults in communal responses to the crisis. Children marched in the streets, raised money for soldiers, spoke out on crucial issues, and became symbols of patriotism. And some, swept up by the growing militarism that inevitably seized many Northern communities, sought to make even more direct—and dramatic—contributions to the war effort.

CHAPTER FIVE

The Militarization of Northern Children

🖎 "ONLY A FEW YEARS AGO," began the August 1862 issue of the *Student and Schoolmate*, "a considerable portion of our population in New England, and perhaps in nearly all the Northern States, looked with a feeling bordering upon contempt on military matters." To most people, soldiers "were simply men engaged in boy's play, and a military company was a senseless pageant to be enjoyed only by little boys and stupid men." A man in uniform strolling down a street in Boston would be "set . . . down as a man with more vanity than brains." Throughout Massachusetts, politicians, editors, and ministers "all vied with each other to see which could get up the smartest satire upon soldiers and military parades." Some suggested abolishing the entire military system.

All that changed, of course, after the attack on Fort Sumter, when "the military spirit rose to a tremendous pitch of enthusiasm" and "the people, as a whole, began to realize the value of a soldier, and a uniform was a sure passport to respect and consideration." Oliver Optic, the editor of this well-respected and widely read magazine, shrugged off the possibility that the nation might become too militaristic. He noted approvingly the "great many companies of juvenile soldiers" in and near Boston, including "a whole battalion of boys" under the command of a fourteen-year-old major that "marched with a steadiness and precision that would have done honor to a regiment of regulars." The article went on to applaud the U.S. army's development of skill over sheer brawn, and highlighted the technological improvements in the weapons of war, from rifled cannon and ironclad boats to breech-loading rifles, siege mortars, and various forms of shell and shot. "The military spirit is in the ascendant now," proclaimed Optic, "and while we hope there will not be too much of it, we trust there will always be enough of it to furnish good soldiers in abundance to defend all our cherished institutions."[1]

Few authors would have dared suggest that it was appropriate to train youngsters in the art of war, even to defend the "cherished institutions" and rights enjoyed by citizens of the United States that were featured prominently in antebellum children's literature and schoolbooks. But the influence of the war on civilian culture, the demands made by the war on families, and the response of Northern communities to the crisis conditioned Northern children to accept—to invite, in fact—the wide-ranging militarization of their lives. In many ways, children who had taken part in war-related community events were, like their parents, simply applying prewar notions to wartime needs. The martial images, rhetoric, and assumptions that came to shape every aspect of children's lives raised their participation in the war to unprecedented—and for some, even dangerous—levels. The militarization of children's play, literature, and vocabulary, and the widespread acceptance by Northerners of youthful volunteers to the army, were the most intense manifestations of the war spirit that invaded virtually every Northern home.

Marshaling the Children

A far-flung effort to mobilize children for the home-front war effort suggests how greatly military terminology and martial attitudes came to dominate wartime discourse, even in the context of children's roles. When a Chicagoan named Alfred L. Sewell sought to draw children into fund-raising for Chicago's Northwestern Sanitary Fair in May 1865, he established the "Army of the American Eagle." Sewell later explained that he had been trying to think of a way to "marshal the children . . . and give them a chance to show how well they love their country and her brave defenders." He recruited youngsters to sell "beautiful Album pictures in oil colors" of "Old Abe," the "War Eagle." Found in the wilds of western Wisconsin before the war, the bird had been adopted by the Eighth Wisconsin, accompanying the regiment through numerous battles and becoming a national celebrity. Everything the children did was couched in military terms. Boys and girls alike became "privates" by buying pictures for a dime each. Recruits were then supposed to organize clubs and sell copies of the pictures to other patriotic children and adults. As children sold more pictures, they advanced through the "ranks" of Sewell's "army," starting with a corporal's rank for selling ten copies and progressing up to major general for selling four thousand copies. Other incentives included gold, silver, and bronze medals for top salesmen and saleswomen, and a copy of the Old Abe booklet for every "colonel" and "general." Each recruit received an "officer's commission" from the "Head-Quarters[,] Army of the American Eagle," decorated with pictures of soldiers and, of course, Old Abe. The inscription spoke of the "Special Trust and Confidence" of the "officer in command" (Sewell) in the "Loyalty and Patriotism" of the children receiving the commission. The back of the commission explained army regulations and encouraged boys and girls to "go into this work like soldiers"; all would act as "recruiting officers," encouraging their friends and their friends' friends to participate. Eventually, Sewell's army of twelve thousand children raised well over $16,000.[2]

It Was Glorious

The ultimate war experience for Civil War children occurred, of course, when they came face to face with armies. Unlike Southern children, most Northern youths could not experience the thrill of battle firsthand, but when Confederates invaded Pennsylvania in the summer of 1863, a few boys and girls got the chance to "see the elephant," as the soldiers called it. Because it was a brief encounter—unlike the protracted sieges that children in Atlanta, Vicksburg, and Petersburg endured—they embraced it with childlike wonder, thrilled with the mixture of danger and excitement and the unknown. They had long read about the war, of course, and had formed their own opinions about the enemy. A boy attending school in Carlisle wrote of the rumors of "town-burnings, or horrible massacres, of treacherous surrenders" in the bloody border warfare in Kansas and Missouri; these images no doubt shaped the anticipated approach of the bloodthirsty Confederates. One ten-year-old, peering through shutters from the safety of his house, thought Jubal Early's division looked like "a wild west show." Other boys, edging closer to the Confederates' camp near Gettysburg, discovered "the feeling of protective comradeship that nice men show to little boys" and ended up chatting and bartering with the grizzled Southerners occupying their town.[3]

The memoirists who had experienced the battle of Gettysburg as children spent little time relating their idle chitchat with the invaders. Many years after the events they still marveled at their good fortune in witnessing the greatest battle of the war. Oddly, a number of parents placed no restrictions on at least a few boys' "goings and comings," and groups of ten- and twelve-year-old boys roamed the battlefield, clambering up hilltops or fences from which to watch units double-quick into battle, artillery batteries deploy into firing lines, and Confederates and Yankees skirmish through and around the town. Many were frightened, but most no doubt agreed with Billy Bayly, who exclaimed, "to me as a boy it was glorious!"[4]

The transition from the excitement of war to its grimmest reality took only a few days or even hours. Tillie Pierce and her friends welcomed Gen. John Buford's cavalry as it trotted through Gettysburg by singing the chorus of "Our Union Forever" over and over (they could not remember the words of all the verses), and "felt amply repaid when we saw that our efforts were appreciated." The troopers' "countenances brightened and we received their thanks and cheers." Later, after evacuating the town for a safer spot behind the lines, Tillie would thrill to the site of artillery units galloping dramatically toward the fighting. Suddenly one of the caissons blew up, and a terribly wounded man was carried into the house where she was staying. "As they pass by I see his eyes are blown out and his whole person seems to be one black mass." He later died.[5]

The Yankees' initial response to the fighting that suddenly surrounded them was a little naive. The McCreary family had watched the Eleventh and Twelfth Corps march through and around town to take up positions west of Gettysburg on Seminary Ridge, and their son Albertus had actually followed the Union forces until Confederate artillery shells began landing too close for comfort. Yet the family sat down to their noon meal as usual. But their food would soon turn cold, for before they were finished "there was so much noise and racket in the street" that they left the table to see what was going on. They saw the street "full of Union soldiers, running and pushing each other, sweaty and black from powder and dust." They distributed water to a few, but when they suddenly realized that hand-to-hand fighting was taking place half a block from their house, they retired to the cellar. They crouched there fearfully as shadows darted past the tiny cellar windows, listening as Confederate soldiers shouted to one another—"Shoot that fellow going over the fence"—and as the combat intensified and a cannon was unlimbered and fired next to their house. Another family who took shelter in their cellar was soon joined by retreating Yankees. Exhausted and wounded men "kept pouring into the cellar until it was so close & offensive from the blood and water on the muddy floor that we could hardly endure it." When the fighting waned, Confederates burst into the McCreary cellar looking for Union soldiers. They found thirteen Yankees hiding under beds, in closets, and under the piano. Before they left, soldiers on both sides sat down together for the dinner offered them by Mr. McCreary. "Now that they had stopped fighting, both sides seemed to be on the best of terms, and laughed and chatted like old comrades."[6]

Like the McCrearys, many Gettysburg children handed out cups of water to the sweating Yankees retreating through town, but others also helped mothers and older sisters care for wounded soldiers, and carried guns and other equipment for weary warriors. During and after the battle, Albertus and his brothers gave their beds to wounded soldiers and slept on the floor or at the Sanitary Commission headquarters. They surveyed the incredible wreckage left by the battle: the broken and abandoned equipment, thousands of dead horses, and wrecked fields and fences. And, of course, with dead horses and humans broiling under the July heat, "the stench from the battle-field . . . was so bad that every one went about with a bottle of pennyroyal or peppermint oil." Albertus hung about the military hospital for hours, sitting on a fence watching surgeons at work on the wretched victims of the battle. "I must say," he confessed, "I got pretty well hardened to such sights." But most Gettysburg children did not concentrate on the human tragedy so much as the excitement and drama. They descended on the battlefield after the Confederate retreat, grabbing souvenirs—knapsacks, abandoned weapons, bits of uniforms, the papers and photographs blown out of men's pockets that littered the field and town—and collecting spent bullets to sell. The debris left behind by the great battle was a bonanza to boys enamored of military-style play. "Almost every boy had a can of powder" salvaged from unfired shells and cartridges, recalled Albertus, which they used to fire abandoned rifles they had also salvaged. They particularly liked to load the guns, leaving the ramrods in the gun barrel, and shoot them into the air. "I often wonder why more boys were not injured." Some were. Albertus was present when a friend, pounding a shell on a rock to shake the powder out of it, struck a spark that exploded the pile of powder. The other boys carried the badly wounded and unconscious schoolmate to his home, but he died within the hour. On another occasion, a year after the battle, Albertus was witness to another horrible accident when he heard an explosion and turned around to see "a young schoolmate lying on his back with his bowels blown away. He looked at me for a second, then closed his eyes in death." A man standing nearby was "almost torn to pieces, his hands hanging in shreds."[7]

What Dreadful Times

Most Northern children did not witness the real war, of course, but sometimes their rhetoric suggests they had. A story sent by a mother to *The Little Pilgrim* described her little girl falling and scraping her head, knees, and arms. While preparing for bed that evening, she looked at her various "wounds" and said to her mother, "Oh dear! What dreadful times these war times are!" The artist Howard Pyle, who later became famous for his illustrations of pirate and war stories, started out by painting a watercolor of a Zouave waving an American flag with one hand and lunging toward a Confederate with a sword in the other. The caption shouted "Ded! Ded! Ded is the 'cesioner!"[8]

Pyle may have picked up at least some of his bloodthirsty enthusiasm for war from the literature produced for children between 1861 and 1865. Although prewar novels and magazines had avoided war entirely, once hostilities began, writers and editors rallied to the Union cause, both politically and militarily. One boy's diary suggests how fully the war changed Northern children's reading material. Gerald Norcross, who turned seven just before the war began,

The Civil War–era children's magazine most influenced by the war was *The Little Corporal,* whose masthead featured a heavily armed young boy dressed in a Zouave uniform. *(The Little Corporal, July 1865)*

recorded his ambitious reading program in a terse diary. For the first couple years of the war, he read traditional children's books like Jacob Abbott's famous "Rollo" books: *Rollo at Play, Rollo at School, Rollo's Vacation, Rollo's Travels.* But in 1863 he checked out *The Little Drummer,* and for the next two years he increasingly consumed books—fiction as well as nonfiction—related to the war: the admiring *Life and Campaigns of Gen. McClellan,* C. C. Coffin's *Days and Nights on the Battlefield* and *Following the Flag,* and dime novels with evocative names like *War Trails, Vicksburg Spy,* and *Old Hal Williams; or the Spy of Atlanta.*[9]

Biographies of generals and descriptions of soldiers' lives became staples in children's magazines and in books published for children. Oliver Optic printed two long series on military affairs in the *Student and Schoolmate* that informed readers in a very detailed fashion how an army worked: how a regiment, brigade, and corps were organized; how a unit set up camp and deployed for battle; the responsibilities of the officers, from the paperwork they completed to their position on the battlefield; and the daily experiences of common soldiers in camp and in combat.[10]

Even the simplest genre of publications for children—the alphabets that taught toddlers their letters with the help of catchy rhymes—was enlisted on behalf of the war effort. Published in 1864, the red, white, and blue *Union ABC* delivered an alphabetical listing of martial sights and ideas. From "A is America, land of the free, B is a Battle our soldiers did see" to "Z is for Zouave, who charged on the foe," the little book portrayed the war for the youngest readers, with entries covering homely soldiers' items like hardtack and knapsack, the inevitable racial stereotype "J is for Jig, which the Contrabands dance," and the harsh "T is a Traitor, that was hung on a tree."[11]

Military images and values infiltrated prewar formats, sometimes with jarring results. A poem celebrating the Union heroes at Ball's Bluff—a small but disastrous affair remembered only because it was one of the first fights of the war—declared, "All hail, ye gallant braves! / Who to your bloody graves / Went 'mid the clash of steel and scream of the shell . . . Howling in spite and joy as ye fell." Vengeance—hardly a value touted in prewar children's literature— would come, however, as for every son of Massachusetts who fell, a hundred would take their place, "Battling till treason is crushed in its gore!"[12]

A popular game in children's magazines of the time was the "Charade," in which clues led readers to guess a certain word or phrase. Normally innocuous, one wartime charade in *The Little Pilgrim* featured a poem:

The drums are beating, fifes are calling;
In haste prepare, my first is near!
Brave men will soon be thickly falling,

While fighting for their country dear.
They madly rush into the fray,
And 'Victory!' soon they loudly shout;
They've won my second—gained the day,
And put the dastard foes to route;
The wounded men alone are dying,
Upon my whole, after the fight;
The slain in bloody heaps are lying,
Making a sad and sick'ning sight.

The answer—just in time for the May 1864 bloodbath in the Wilderness—was "a battlefield."[13]

Prewar magazines had frequently written approvingly of good boys and girls minding their parents, contributing to charity, displaying all those values and attitudes cherished by the middle class. But during the war, young soldiers—boys, really—were frequently held up as models for youthful emulation as they cheerfully and determinedly went about the business of killing. The nondenominational religious magazine *The Little Pilgrim* approvingly reported a thirteen-year-old's steadfast conduct on a Mississippi River gunboat: he stayed at his post, passing ammunition to a gun crew, until his boat sank under him. He survived, and the *Pilgrim* commented, "So young a lad, so brave and cool in danger, will make himself known" as he grew older.[14]

Those were exactly the characteristics that authors of war stories for children and youth gave to their young heroes. Teenagers appeared as cool, calculating, and competent soldiers and sailors, rising through the ranks to become junior officers with startling responsibilities and opportunities for personal glory. Oliver Optic produced a pair of trilogies—immensely popular and reissued several times before 1900—that followed the military careers of twin seventeen-year-olds Tom (who joined the army) and Jack (who joined the

A is America, land of the free.

B is a Battle, our soldiers did see.

Even the archetypal children's genre, the ABC book, was recruited to the Northern war effort. *(The Union ABC, 1864)*

navy) Somers. The boys represented everything that Americans could want in a young man. Optic described Tom's story as "a narrative of personal adventure, delineating the birth and growth of pure patriotism in the soul of the hero," who was a "true soldier, one who loves his country, and fights for her because he loves her; but, at the same time, one who is true to himself and his God."[15]

Most of Tom's and Jack's qualities would have made them the perfect antebellum teenagers: their piety, ambition, and sense of responsibility would have been appropriate for the heroes of any children's story or book before the war. But wartime demanded that other qualities emerge from the American character—fighting skills, the willingness to die for a cause, leadership—and the Somers boys owned those qualities in spades. Both boys thrive in the military, succeeding as leaders of small squads of colorful sidekicks, taking part in major military operations, and operating behind enemy lines. Although they never become totally comfortable with the idea of killing, they also refuse to shy away from the duty. In *The Yankee Middy*, in a story line that would never have appeared in an antebellum juvenile magazine, Jack leads the crew of his small gunboat into a hand-to-hand fight to the death with a band of Confederate smugglers. Jack mortally wounds the Rebel leader—who also happened to be his rival for the hand of an attractive young lady—and his men save the day. In his first big fight—which appears in *The Sailor Boy*, the first of the set—Jack kills a Rebel with a pistol. Afterward his lip trembles and his face goes pale—but the youngster apparently grows more stern; he rarely has second thoughts about killing in subsequent actions (though he does temper his warlike nature in *The Yankee Middy*, comforting his dying enemy by reading the Bible to him).

In the final entry of his trilogy, Tom has risen to the rank of major—primarily through battlefield promotions recognizing his uncommon bravery and fighting abilities—and his story ends with marriage (Jack appears at the wedding with a girl on his arm too).

Optic provides a kind of benediction to the series: "Major Somers is a man of good motives, and of high Christian principles, won in the day of trial and suffering, no less than in prosperity; and we doubt not he will be as true to his God, his country, and himself, in the future, as he has been in the past; when, by his fidelity, his bravery, and his patriotism, he carved out his fortunes on the battle-fields of the Great Rebellion." At the time, Tom is barely twenty-one![16]

Other literary representations of teenage soldiers show similar transitions from eager, earnest young boys to steely-eyed officers. Frank Nelson, a young acting master's mate on a Mississippi River gunboat, punishes a family of Confederate women who refuse to lower their Confederate flag by burning down their house. "Frank could not help pitying the women, who were thus obliged to stand by and witness the destruction of their home. But he knew that they had brought it on themselves, and that they deserved it; and, besides, he had only done his duty, for he was acting under orders." He later kills a Confederate with a bayonet.[17]

Playing at War

Just as publishers for children fit their products to wartime needs, so too did manufacturers of toys and games. Serious issues barely skimmed the surface of their products, which for the most part merely introduced certain war themes and a highly generic brand of patriotism. Some had fairly serious, even realistic approaches to the war, but many sought only to offer mildly informative pastimes. If children gleaned some small amount of patriotic inspiration from playing with them, it was a welcome but relatively unintended by-product. In decks of cards, eagles, shields, stars, and flags substituted for the traditional suits; colonels replaced kings, the Goddess of Liberty replaced queens, and majors replaced jacks. Cheap and easy-to-understand mazes were easily transformed into wartime games like "Running the Blockade." Mechanical dolls developed before the war were made up to look like Zouaves or even the infamous Gen. Benjamin Butler, and popular lithographs of war scenes were cut into jigsaw puzzles.

A broad sense of humor characterized a fairly elaborate board game called *A Visit to Camp*, which offered a lighthearted look at army life. Players took the parts of caricatures like a rather foppish captain, a hard-drinking sutler, a Zouave, a bewhiskered colonel, a hapless surgeon, a cross-eyed, rotund musician, and a *vivandier* (in a feminized Zouave uniform). A unique and unusually politicized item was an automated toy that presented Abraham Lincoln as an organ grinder and a fiddle-playing monkey who bore more than a passing resemblance to Gideon Welles, secretary of the navy.

Even objects not necessarily produced for children became popular among them. The *Philadelphia Ledger & Transcript* reported early in the war that "most" of the city's shops were prominently displaying "articles, either useful or ornamental, growing out of the Union feeling of the war," including soldiers' equipment, hats and caps, neckties and collars decorated with stars and stripes, as well as military books and manuals. Helping prepare children for the military parades they would doubtless watch, the United States Flag Company in Chicago advertised "Four Sizes of Toy Flags from One to Four Feet in Length." Just in time for Christmas 1863, one children's book advertised "Fifty lithographed games and Twenty Four Lithographed Picture Books," paper soldiers, the "Eastern Army Guide" and the "General Army Guide of southern territory," the "Glorious Union Packet," bird's-eye maps of Southern territory and battlefields, "Grand Battle Tableaux " of Gettysburg, Pea Ridge, and Second Manassas, pictures of camps and hospitals, and brightly illustrated and patriotic note paper and envelopes.[18]

Even the presents that Northern children (and their mothers) implored Yankee soldiers to send home from the front had a decidedly militaristic character. Guns and swords abandoned on battlefields, parts of Union or Confederate uniforms, scraps of shrapnel, and other bits and pieces of the debris of war found their way into countless Northern homes. Some men personalized the gifts by sending miníe balls that had crashed into nearby trees or breast-works, or rings shaped from shell fragments, or splinters from battle-scarred ships. An Illinois officer sent home a double-barreled shotgun fired at him by a Confederate soldier at Fort Donelson, while another father forwarded a spent bullet that slammed into his chest at Fredericksburg. A small fashion trend emerged when boys began sewing on their clothes badges representing their fathers' divisions in the Army of the Potomac.[19]

Warlike interests joined more traditional peaceful pursuits in the crowded bedroom of one little girl. On the door hung a sign reading "The Devil's Den: No Admittunse Except on Bisiness." Inside she crowded all the possessions and objects she had acquired over the years. Pictures of Civil War generals, battle scenes from *Harper's Weekly*, a flintlock pistol, a bayonet, and a cavalry sword were featured—this was toward the end of the Civil War—and tacked on the walls or scattered on shelves around the room were "any odds or ends" she had encountered or been given: bird's nests (and the branches on which they had been built), "bits of Florida moss," arrowheads, interesting stones, and her books, which ranged from the Bible and *The Pilgrim's Progress* to *The Swiss Family Robinson* and a volume of infantry tactics.[20]

Although some girls were interested in the martial side of war, boys, not surprisingly, took a special interest in bringing the war into their play. As soon as the war began, Julia Dent Grant recalled, while "the men were holding meetings and calling for volunteers," the boys in Galena, Illinois, "were playing at war, wearing military caps, beating small drums, guarding the crossings, and demanding countersigns." A Boston boy and a friend created huge armies of paper soldiers, which carried out foraging expeditions and fought elaborate battles—"we would blow sometimes as our volleys and then retreat for a while and then count . . . the number killed." On another occasion the boys took turns blindfolding themselves and poking a "very sharp knife" at the soldiers; the figures struck by the knife were considered casualties.[21]

A group of boys living on the south bank of the Ohio River went several steps further. Within days of the Confederate attack on Fort Sumter, they "got busy building Fort Sumters" out of mud and wooden blocks, with clothespin soldiers manning the ramparts. They fashioned cannon from old brass pistol barrels attached to blocks of wood. Charged with a little powder and loaded with pebbles, the blasts shattered the little forts and created "terrible slaughter" among the wooden soldiers. The president of the new Confederacy also became a target when the boys made proxy Jefferson Davises out of potatoes and sticks and blew them up with firecrackers. Rather less violent but much more famous was the boys' company organized in the White House. Tad and Willie Lincoln's "Mrs. Lincoln's Zouaves" was reviewed on at least one occasion by the commander-in-chief himself. The boys also mounted a log cannon on the White House roof and frequently court-martialed a Zouave doll, which they would then execute and bury with full military honors.[22]

Some girls shared their brothers' military ambitions. A self-proclaimed tomboy from Yonkers, New York, so loved her brother's colorful Zouave uniform that she vainly tried to convince him to take her along when he went to his regiment. Undaunted, she obtained a soldiers' cap, canteen, and drum and practiced beating it as she marched "up and down the path in front of our house . . . until every head in the street must have ached." When she thought herself ready for service, she made the day-long trip into the city, by herself, to meet the colonel of her brother's unit, hoping he would make her "daughter of the regiment." He declined, however, and when she returned home her worried and angry parents sent her off to bed. "But I made a tent of my sheets, and with a broom for a musket, drilled myself till I was so tired that I fell asleep."[23]

Girls turned military concerns into gender-appropriate play. In this illustration from Louisa May Alcott's "Nelly's Hospital," the title character searches for patients for her army hospital. *(Our Young Folks, April 1865)*

But martial dreams were rare among girls, and their application of the war to their play normally followed more traditional gender lines, though these "safe" forms of play were sometimes applied to wartime scenarios. In a famous short story published in *Our Young Folks* just after the war, Louisa May Alcott portrays Nelly, a little girl whose wounded brother—home for an extended medical furlough—inspires her to do something for the war effort. She decides to honor her brother's sacrifice and do good for her neighborhood by building a hospital for wounded animals. She and the gardener's son set up a hospital in an old outbuilding, and she proceeds to gather patients from the yard and in nearby fields and forests. This is not so unusual for children of any place or time, but Nelly organizes her hospital as a military installation, builds an "ambulance" emblazoned with the Sanitary Commission emblem, and collects and treats, among other unfortunate creatures, a fly trapped in a spider web (she calls it a "black contraband") and a grey snake (obviously a captured "rebel").[24]

Such Boys Make Men

Although a common perception is that hundreds of thousands of soldiers in both armies were under the minimum age of eighteen set by Congress in August 1861 (boys younger than eighteen could enlist with their parents' permission), those numbers are greatly exaggerated. Bell I. Wiley found that only 1.6 percent of a sampling of more than 14,000 Union soldiers were officially under the age of eighteen, and although he admits that the number was probably higher—many youngsters simply lied about their age to recruiters who were not particularly selective—the percentage of underage soldiers certainly did not reach the 10 or 20 percent estimated by at least one historian. Still, a chilling number of truly young boys appeared on the rosters of Union army regiments. A statistician for the Sanitary Commission, who studied the records of more than a million Yankees, found 10,233 under the age of eighteen, including 127 thirteen-year-olds.[25]

Underaged boys who enlisted in the army sometimes did so despite older brothers' warnings. Harvey White Magee turned sixteen in the fall of 1863 and desperately wanted to join up. Every time he mentioned it in a letter to his brother Tom, who was already in the army, the older boy would "always answer . . . expressing tender affection for me, and encouraging me in my patriotism for our country, but would enumerate the hardships attending and endured by the soldiers, and always ending his letters in appealing to me to remain at home and assist our father on the farm." Just before the end of the war, Jasper Barrett wrote to his mother from a New Orleans hospital urging his younger brother Marion not to enlist. Soldiering was fine "while a fellow has good health but let him get sick and see where he is . . . he haint got mother to make tea for him and wait on him."[26]

Despite the absence of mothers in the military, many Northern boys ached to get into the army, to get as close to the action as possible, to share the great national purpose of saving the Union. Enraged by the Baltimore mob's attack on the Sixth Massachusetts in the first days of the conflict, ten-year-old Henry Cabot Lodge immediately decided to become a drummer, for he "had gathered from my reading that such was the proper and conventional thing for a boy to do." He failed to convince his father, however, and had to settle for "imagining desperate assaults and gallant exploits, from which I always escaped alive and glorious, a soothing exercise in which I frequently indulged" at bedtime.[27]

As soon as President Lincoln called for troops in April 1861, a trio of under-ten-year-olds from Cambridge, Massachusetts, marched grandly into an army recruiting station and offered their services to the nation. One of the boys' younger brother reported that the officer in charge "received the lads with gravity, examined their eyes, noses, teeth, made them strip to the skin and thumped them," then sent them to another office, where the unusually thorough—for Civil War–era armies—physical examination was repeated and where, as a last humiliating straw, they were finally rejected. A Wisconsin youngster tried to enlist at a war meeting held in the log-house school he attended as a sixteen-year-old; his father quickly stepped in to foil his patriotic effort, embarrassing him and inspiring his sister to call him "a little snotty boy." Mortified, he kept trying to enlist and finally did so with the help of the father of a friend, who was a captain in the army. At least one teenager, an Ohio seventeen-year-old with two older brothers already in the army, was so depressed when his parents refused to give him permission to join up that he hanged himself.[28]

Other boys succeeded in enlisting. After spending many long afternoons with Gerald Norcross fighting extended battles and conducting "foraging" expeditions with armies of paper soldiers, a fifteen-year-old Boston boy crossed the line between imaginary and actual war when he lied about his age, took an alias, and joined a local regiment. After a few panic-stricken weeks, his father found him and retrieved him from the army unharmed. Once home, he and Gerald picked up where they had left off in their imaginary battles.[29]

Other boys did not return home. Ernest Wardwell, who before the war had frequently fought imaginary battles and had himself organized a boys' company, joined the mob attacking the Sixth Massachusetts as it marched through Baltimore. Although he started the day an ardent Southerner, the Yankees' "gallant bearing" impressed him, and he eventually jumped into the marching column and volunteered to carry a Massachusetts sergeant's rifle. Swept along with the regiment as it was attacked and then returned fire, the teenager ended up enlisting and rising to the rank of captain.[30]

The *Union ABC's* entry for "D" was "Drummer Boy, called little Ben," and Americans of all ages loved to hear about the youngest heroes, the drummer boys whose job it was to signal troop movements. They were among the many young boys listed as "musicians" in the Union and Confederate armies. Although there was no apparent minimum age for musicians during the first three years of the war, in March 1864 Congress prohibited the enlistment of anyone under sixteen. In the meantime, however, scores if not hundreds of boys under the age of fourteen served as drummers, and a few eleven years old and younger also served.[31]

C. W. Bardeen of Massachusetts, an avid and pint-sized abolitionist and Republican before the war, was thirteen when Fort Sumter was fired on. The crisis caused him no end of worry. "I remember walking up and down the sitting room, puffing out my breast as though the responsibility rested on my poor little shoulders, shaking my fist at the south, and threatening her with dire calamities." He joined the boys' company at his grammar school and took fencing lessons. His first attempt to enlist as a drummer failed; a relative of his stepfather's took him to see the infamous Gen. Benjamin Butler, who took one look at him and declared, "Take the damned little snip away, we've got babies enough in this brigade already." Undaunted, and with help from a cousin who happened to be a recruiting sergeant, a few months later he managed to get into the First Massachusetts as a musician. He served about two years. Other drummers were even younger. Edward Black became a drummer in the Twenty-first Indiana at the age of eight and served for nearly the entire war. Eight drummers in a single regiment, the Second Connecticut Heavy Artillery, were no more than fifteen years old; at least two were killed in action before war's end.[32]

The most famous drummer of them all, John Clem, ran away from home more than a month before the First Battle of Bull Run and tried to join a company in the Third Ohio. The captain dismissed the tiny nine-year-old by saying he "wasn't enlisting infants." Clem attached himself to another regiment, the Twenty-second Michigan, and even though he was not officially on the roll, the officers took up a collection to pay his thirteen-dollar-a-month wage. When Clem's drum was smashed a year later at Shiloh, he took to carrying a gun (by that time he was a regular member of the regiment) and used it to shoot a Confederate colonel who demanded his surrender at Chickamauga. He became a celebrity and a sergeant after that exploit, and continued to serve as a messenger. He was twice wounded before the war ended.[33]

In those days before public schools had music classes or choirs, and when most families had neither the money nor the space for drum sets, pianos, or other musical instruments, few boys knew how to play a drum, bugle, or fife when they entered the army. C. W. Bardeen admitted that although he practiced for hours on a borrowed drum, "I have never succeeded in anything less than in learning to drum." He was relieved when, after several futile months, he switched to the fife. While the men spent their days learning the manual of arms and how to march into a line of battle, drummers and other musicians practiced for hours on end. Their jobs were important, for every aspect of soldiers' lives was accompanied by music. Drummers and buglers gave commands on the battlefield but also signaled when it was time to get up, time to drill, time to water horses, and time to go to bed. Some performed other duties too, from digging ditches to delivering mail to building roads. The drummer of the 104th Ohio worked in camp as a barber, carried water, maintained the surgeon's instruments, buried the dead, and drew maps. Another made a small fortune—at least for a boy in the 1860s—by selling pastries and fruit to soldiers. The most common chore was helping carry wounded men from the battlefield and assisting surgeons in field hospitals. A sixteen-year-old musician from Maine filled the crucial role of applying ether to patients undergoing amputations and, afterward, carrying the arms and legs to a nearby trench for burial.[34]

One stereotype of the drummer boys' existence was that they were treated as pets by their comrades. A soldier in the Twenty-second Wisconsin wrote his little brother about Johnnie Walker, the regiment's twelve-year-old drummer. Whenever the regimental band played, townspeople would treat Johnny with apples and cake. Although on the march the "always singing and laughing" Johnnie normally kept up with the "big men," when he tired one of the officers would often dismount and let Johnnie ride. Johnnie was very popular among the soldiers "because he is a good little boy, is always pleasant and polite and"—this may have been a subtle hint that the soldier's brother should watch his own behavior—"not saucy like a great many boys."[35]

Such favoritism often appeared on those unfortunate occasions when a drummer died of disease or wounds. Clarence McKenzie, mortally wounded in a parade ground accident barely a month after Fort Sumter, was memorialized in a reverent little biography published by the Board of Publication of the Reformed Protestant

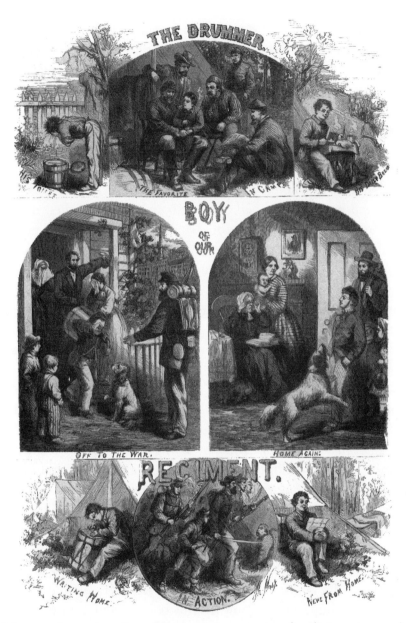

The popular conception of drummers as mascots for their regiments is central to this wartime illustration from *Harper's Weekly*. (*Harper's Weekly, December 19, 1863*)

Dutch Church. He was remembered by comrades—who had only known him a few weeks—"as a pious, dear little fellow" who never went to sleep "without reading his Bible and saying his prayers." He was good-natured, "kind and obliging," and everyone in the regiment "loved him, as their feelings showed after he was shot." But for every drummer boy who became the center of attention were several who seemed to have been treated no differently than any other infantryman.[36]

Indeed, boy soldiers and drummers experienced all the disease, filth, and hard living experienced by their older comrades, not to mention the intemperance, propensity for gambling, irreligious attitudes, and general bad habits of many other soldiers. One fifteen-year-old musician won $120 in an evening of gambling. Even the boy editors of the Newark High School *Athenaeum* presented the corruption of soldiers as a commonplace. An editorial supporting the work of the U.S. Christian Commission explained that, since most soldiers were "ready for every kind of fun and adventure" and, in camp, left with the kind of "idle time" that is a "source of evil," one should not be surprised that, "surrounded as he is by temptation of nearly every description, he often returns from the battlefield ruined as to all that is virtuous and religious."[37]

In *Frank Manly, the Drummer Boy*, the well-known children's author J. T. Trowbridge acknowledged the moral corruption that boys faced. Frank's mother admits that "there is one danger I should dread for you worse than the chances of the battlefield . . . That you might be led away by bad company." She worries about soldiers who are "not such persons as I would wish to have you on very intimate terms with." "To have you become corrupted by their evil influences," she continues, still trying to talk her son out of his patriotic enthusiasm, "to know that my boy was no longer the pure, truthful child he was; that he would blush to have his sisters know his habits and companions; to see him come home, if he ever does, reckless and dissipated—O, I could endure any thing, even his death, better than that." Frank, pained that his mother might think his resistance to corruption could be so weak, declares, "you shall hear of my death, before you hear of my drinking, or gambling, or swearing, or any thing of the kind." He seals his vow by writing his promise on a blank leaf of his New Testament. Nevertheless, not long after he arrives at his regiment Frank succumbs to the soldierly temptations of drink and playing cards. He recovers and reforms other soldiers along with himself, but most situations like these were not so easily resolved.[38]

C. W. Bardeen admitted to his diary on a drizzly New Year's Day 1864 that his year in the army had not had a positive effect on his character. "I bear witness to its contaminating effects. Many an evil habit has sprung up in me since Jan 1st, 1863. God grant that the year on which we have now entered be not so." The career of this drummer turned fifer would in fact have inspired most parents to keep their sons at home. C. W. barely mentioned religion—though he did go to church from time to time, he "was not much inter-ested" in the only Bible class he attended—and, though professing to have signed the temperance pledge, he eventually came to enjoy his occasional ration of whiskey. He was arrested and very briefly confined to the guardhouse when he failed to obey orders. Bardeen was on his own much of the time, from when he left his home in Boston to go to the front to when his regiment approached the shell-shattered town of Fredericksburg in their first big battle, to when he had to make his own shelter in winter quarters. The vice he came to love the most was gambling. He frequently played a card game called Bluff, and though Bardeen the reminiscing senior citi-zen knew the evils of the sporting life, the teenaged musician could not get enough of it. During the month following the battle of Chancellorsville, Bardeen's brief diary entries mention playing Bluff ten times, sometimes "all day." He won a few times, but his losses mounted throughout the month, totaling over thirty dollars by early June. One day he lost a whopping twenty dollars; "no comment is needed," he wrote in his diary. His penchant for high-stakes card playing would cost him later in the year, when his regiment was stationed for a time in New York City. After he fell in with a group of New York soldiers—from whom he won fifty dollars one night— he ended up being "cleaned out" by the losing players, who tore his vest and took all his money.[39]

Literary representations of boy soldiers normally showed them triumphing over temptation. Tom Somers—the seventeen-year-old "Soldier Boy" of Oliver Optic's famous trilogy—survived First Manassas, was captured twice by Confederates, and endured hard living in the Shenandoah Valley. But Tom had to fight "a greater battle than that in which he had been engaged at Bull Run a hundred times, in resisting the temptations which beset him from within and without. True to God and true to himself, he had won the victory," despite being surrounded by gamblers, drinkers, and oath-swearers.[40]

No one could shorten the hard marches or improve the awful rations that even the youngest drummers shared with their older comrades. Even "Captain George, the Drummer-Boy," a novella by the children's writer M. E. Dodge, which generally presents the heroic side of war, paints a pretty grim picture of the daily life of drummers and soldiers. Fourteen-year-old George is recruited by an officer who hears him drumming with his boys' company, and he goes on to carry dispatches to General Pope for his wounded captain and to rally the troops by furiously drumming from an exposed rock at Antietam. He comes to know the men in his unit as "jaded, weary men, dust-soiled and nearly dust-choked"; they are veterans, not "picture-soldiers." George has learned that "all his former ideas of warfare were soon proved to be very fanciful."[41]

A drummer who kept a diary that he later turned into a kind of regimental history of the Second Minnesota sounds like any other veteran soldier in the attention he pays to the weather, his description of long marches, and his complaints about rations. He witnessed sights that most parents would have protected their children from at all costs, and when he and a friend wandered over the battlefield at Shiloh, the fifteen-year-old realized that "the most terrible scenes of carnage my boyish imagination had ever figured fell far short of the dreadful reality." The boys "beheld a scene of destruction, terrible, indeed, if there ever was one in this wide world. Dismounted gun-carriages, shattered caissons, knapsacks, haversacks, muskets, bayonets, and accoutrements scattered over the field in wildest confusion. Horses—poor creatures—dead and dying, and, worse and most awful of all, dead men by the hundreds." He also worked in the hospital, where one of his jobs was, "every few moments," carrying soldiers who had died to the dead house. He later suffered from chronic dysentery but nevertheless reenlisted with most of the survivors of his regiment. At one point he calculated the miles the Second had marched during its years in the service (971) and estimated that another year with similar casualties from battle and disease would wipe out the regiment. Indeed, after the battle of Missionary Ridge in 1863, only six members of his company were fit for duty. "Such are the horrors of war," he wrote resignedly; this drummer boy could hardly be considered the boy pet of his unit.[42]

The reality of drummer boys' service should have caused their parents to hesitate before allowing their sons to enlist. Fictional drummers are often boys whose fathers have already died in the service of their country and whose mothers' patriotism overcomes their reluctance to allow their sons to leave home. That may have been the case in some real Yankee families, but it was rarely so clear-cut. Clarence McKenzie's parents were deeply divided over the prospect of his joining the army. His mother "had been very much opposed to his going with the regiment," repeatedly expressing her fear "that he would be killed, and she would never see him again." On the other hand, according to Clarence's biographer, his father "had not only been willing, but rather anxious that his son should go.—He knew that this was a favorite regiment—that many good men were going—that it was an honorable post for his little boy to occupy, and that if cut down, he would die in the cause of his country." While his mother could think only of the dangers facing her little boy—"with a woman's and a mother's fear"—his father could think only of the possibility of glory and honor that would come to his son if he survived his contribution to the war effort.[43]

Some parents may have felt that giving up a son to the army was a way to contribute to the war effort, as did the father in a poem published early in the war: "God bless you, then; Such boys make MEN," the father quickly replied when his son asked permission to go. "Take drum in hand, And through the land, Go forth—your country's pride." Others may have assented out of economic desperation. A story that appeared in a reader for young students depicts a twelve- or thirteen-year-old boy brought before the commander of a Union company in Missouri by his mother. Her Unionist husband has been killed and her property destroyed by local Confederates, and "she wanted to find employment for herself and her son." The captain somewhat reluctantly takes little Eddie into his company, where he performs his duty and is, rather inevitably, killed at the Battle of Wilson's Creek.[44]

A slightly older and decidedly less pious boy offered an alternative explanation for why at least a few parents went along with their sons' dreams of martial glory. By the time C. W. Bardeen was thirteen—the year the war began—he had become a "disturbing element" in the household. His father was dead, but his mother had remarried. "I was conceited," he admitted years later, "boastful, self-willed, disobedient, saucy, not lazy but always wanting to do something else than the duty of the moment, absurdly scrupulous in some things yet in others" more likely to lie. In sum, "I was wholly disagreeable." He had been expelled from school at least once and had run away from home to become, briefly, a traveling salesman of pictures of Yankee generals. He believed that, once he had finally gotten into the army, his mother felt "a relief . . . to have me really in the army, under authority that could control me, with the responsibility off her mind."[45]

Although they were not supposed to be combat soldiers, many drummer boys did come in harm's way. One boy in a regiment marching with Sherman through Georgia grew so weary he could not go on; he lay down along the road and was captured by Confederate cavalry. Another teenage soldier with Sherman's army left his Iowa regiment one night and was captured a few miles away and court martialed. He pleaded with the court that he had simply "wanted to see my mother," but he was nonetheless convicted and executed by a firing squad. Charles King, a twelve-year-old whose parents agreed to his enlistment as a drummer only after a captain in the Forty-ninth Pennsylvania promised to take personal responsibility for the boy, was mortally wounded by shrapnel at Antietam and died three painful days later. A Wisconsin boy served as drummer for much of the war; although he was only thirteen when mustered out in 1865, Martin Purcell had seen his share of combat, been captured by Confederates and escaped, and gave useful intelligence to generals in the Army of the Potomac when he staggered back into Union lines after making his way through occupied Petersburg, Virginia. When his regiment mustered out, his comrades gave him a silver shell drum as a token of their admiration.[46]

"The Boy of Chancellorville," a classic tale from the long catalog of war stories published in *Our Young Folks*, is a veritable checklist of the experiences that the parents of drummers and underage soldiers must have feared for their sons. The title character, whose real-life experiences the author purported to describe, is only twelve when his unit enters the horrific fighting in the Wilderness southwest of Washington in May 1863. The story opens with the boy—Robert—in the thick of the fighting until his captain orders him to go to the rear to help with the wounded. For the next several pages, which cover nearly a year in Robert's life, he endures shot and shell, sees men killed and maimed all around him, witnesses the last breath of a brave comrade, is captured and marched off to Libby Prison, is abused by cruel guards, becomes ill and nearly dies, and is finally exchanged and sent home.[47]

Although it was rarer than legend would have it, from time to time boy drummers would throw away their drums, grab rifles, and blast away at the enemy. In fact, at least seventeen drummer boys were awarded the Congressional Medal of Honor. Orion Howe of the Fifty-fifth Illinois delivered an urgent request for more ammunition to Gen. William T. Sherman during the Vicksburg campaign, despite a serious leg wound. Sherman was so impressed he wrote a widely circulated letter to Secretary of War Edwin M. Stanton commending the boy and describing the incident: "I was in the front near the road which formed my line of attack" when "this young lad came up to me, wounded and bleeding," and cried, "Gen. Sherman send some cartridges to Colonel Malmborg, the men are nearly all out." Sherman asked him if he was hurt, and Orion replied, "They shot me in the leg, but . . . send the cartridges right away." Sherman ordered him to the rear at once, and as the boy limped off to the hospital, he called over his shoulder, "caliber 51." Sherman recommended that the War Department reward him with an appointment to the U.S. Naval Academy (he was too young for West Point) and concluded, "I'll warrant that the boy has in him the elements of a man, and I commend him to the Government as one worthy the fostering care of some one of its National institutions."[48]

Newspapers, books, and magazines, for children and adults alike, often featured images and tales of drummer boys, who were the heroes of adventure stories, reformers of grizzled and sinful veterans, and the subject of numerous poems and drawings. Many of these stories told of the heroic deaths of little drummer boys. "The Drummer-Boy's Burial," a poem that appeared in *Harper's New Monthly Magazine* during the bloody summer of 1864 (when, at battles like the Wilderness and Spotsylvania and Cold Harbor, Union forces lost sixty-thousand men in three months), was typical.

Stories, poems, and illustrations of drummer boys dying in the line of duty were a staple of wartime publications. *(Harper's New Monthly Magazine, July 1864)*

In the aftermath of a terrible fight, two girls come upon the body of a young drummer, smiling in death. His "broken drum beside him all his life's short story told: How he did his duty bravely till the death-tide o'er him rolled." The girls do their own duty by burying him and conducting a short, simple funeral service.[49]

Children's publications also featured child heroes. A poem from Oliver Optic's *Student and Schoolmate*, called "The Drummer-Boy of Fort Donelson," according to its author was based on the true story of a fifteen-year-old drummer who survived the fighting at Fort Donelson in February 1862 but who later died from "cold and exhaustion."

No more shook the earth with the cannon's dread thunder;
The shriek and the war-cry clashed wildly no more,
Nor shells, madly bursting, rent columns asunder;
The night had set in, and the battle was o'er.

The weary young drummer-boy saw now before him
No foe on the field, save the dying or slain;
And he sank down to rest, when a slumber came o'er him,
The slumber from which he should wake not again.

He laid himself down, with the dying around him,
The sky for his tent, and the field for his bed;
And there, at the dawn of the morning, we found him,
As lifeless and cold as the stone at his head.

No shot for its victim his young heart had chosen;
Unharmed he had passed through the heat of the fray;
But the cold, wintry night-wind his life's blood had frozen,
And his spirit had passed without murmur away.

His drum and his sabre we buried beside him,
And paid him the honors befitting the brave!
And knew that, though Fate length of days had denied him,
His comrades, in pride, would his memory save.

And there let him rest, on the battle-field fearful,
Where heroes, in thousands, repose at his side;
And we'll think on his doom with a feeling less tearful,
To know that for justice and freedom he died.[50]

Although he survives the amputation of his arm, the hero of the American Tract Society's *Charlie the Drummer Boy* finds himself badly wounded and alone on a battlefield, apparently forgotten by his unit. He crawls to a spring, where, with the characteristic serenity found in most characters in the Sunday School genre, he waits patiently, finding comfort in the cool water and murmuring a prayer of thanks. Parents would give anything, of course, to keep their little boys from such a state, but *Charlie the Drummer* uses the plight of one little boy to explain a higher purpose. Through the long night Charlie ignores his own pain and suffering to calm and feed from his own haversack another wounded man who crawls to the spring. The soldier is rough and profane, lapping up water and tearing like an animal at the food Charlie gives him. A simple question from Charlie—"Say, have you a mother?" ("The kind little fellow in honesty thought / That only an orphan could be so untaught")—awakens a host of memories and regrets in the grizzled veteran, who predicts his death and his journey to "the fiery tortures to which I must go." Charlie assures him that "No sinner need perish, since Jesus has died," and guides him through a battlefield conversion. The long poem ends as Charlie returns home with an empty sleeve but otherwise recovered—accompanied by the man he saved on the battlefield. The family rallies around the crippled little boy, the soldier willingly returns to duty, and the tale ends by comparing the duty that soldiers owe to their officers to the duty that all men and women owe to their God.[51]

"The Boy of Chancellorville" had performed similar good deeds during his time in the army; his kindnesses to wounded men, his good nature, and his apparent ability to cheer up and bring out the best in the hard men he encountered was typical of drummer boys—at least the ones who appeared in magazine articles and novels: "You may think that what such a little fellow did, at such a time, could not be of much consequence to anybody," wrote Edmund Kirke, the author of "The Boy of Chancellorville." "But it was. He saved one or two human lives, and lighted the passage of a score of souls through the dark valley; and so did more than any of our great generals on those bloody days. He saved lives, they destroyed them."[52]

The young patriots who entered the army when they should have been beginning apprenticeships or starting the new high schools springing up in most Northern cities and towns may have gone into the service as boys, but they returned home as men. There was a transition period, of course. That underage soldiers in the Union army were not so far removed from their younger friends and siblings is demonstrated by a series of letters by a group of boys in the Forty-sixth Massachusetts, sent to their former teacher and classmates in Springfield, Massachusetts. "Dear Teacher and friends" or "Dear Teacher and family," they would write, and proceed to pack their letters with information about their first few months in the army, including their sea voyage to New Bern, North Carolina (including details of their seasickness), military routines, and the African Americans they encountered (and were decidedly unimpressed by), along with assurances to Miss Stebbins, their teacher, that they were reading their Bibles. The letters resemble nothing so much as letters from a schoolmate who has moved to a new town or is away on vacation.[53]

A hardening process was inevitable, even for boys such as these. In many ways, underage soldiers ceased to be children long before their eighteenth birthday; the experiences of "ponies," as adult soldiers called the youngest recruits, were indistinguishable from those of older men. And many of these boy veterans took on the attitudes and gravitas of adults. A young Minnesotan who enlisted in the First Minnesota as a fifteen-year-old gradually became a kind of father figure to his fatherless family. He wrote letters filled with advice for his younger brother: "Tell him," he wrote his mother, "he must be a good boy and not trouble his mother as much as I did." When his mother suggested that she might volunteer to become an army nurse, he called himself "the milatary General of our family" and sternly forbade her from going to the army. And after he took a bul-

THE DEAD DRUMMER BOY.

'MIDST tangled roots that lined the wild ravine,
  Where the fierce fight raged hottest through the day,
And where the dead in scattered heaps were seen,
Amid the darkling forests' shade and sheen,
  Speechless in death he lay.

The setting sun, which glanced athwart the place
  In slanting lines, like amber-tinted rain,
Fell sidewise on the drummer's upturned face,
Where Death had left his gory finger's trace
  In one bright crimson stain.

The silken fringes of his once bright eye
  Lay like a shadow on his cheek so fair;
His lips were parted by a long-drawn sigh,
That with his soul had mounted to the sky
  On some wild martial air.

No more his hand the fierce tatoo shall beat,
  The shrill reveillé, or the long roll's call,
Or sound the charge, when in the smoke and heat
Of fiery onset foe with foe shall meet,
  And gallant men shall fall.

Yet maybe in some happy home, that one,
  A mother, reading from the list of dead,
Shall chance to view the name of her dear son,
And move her lips to say, "God's will be done!"
  And bow in grief her head.

But more than this what tongue shall tell his story?
  Perhaps his boyish longings were for fame?
He lived, he died; and so, *memento mori*—
Enough if on the page of War and Glory
  Some hand has writ his name.

Another example of the "dead drummer boy" genre of Civil War poetry.
(Harper's New Monthly Magazine, February 1863)

let in the leg at Gettysburg, he complained like an old soldier about the way changing weather pained his war wound.[54]

C. W. Bardeen seemed not to have minded his lost childhood. "As I read over this diary I am sorry for the little boy who underwent so many privations and sufferings," he wrote in his preface, "but I was not sorry for myself at the time." When most middle-class boys his age would be opening Christmas presents and enjoying holiday feasts, C. W. celebrated his first Christmas in the army in 1862 with a meal of "salt junk & Hard Tack."[55]

That the Northern public accepted—even, in some cases, promoted and glorified—the enlistment of boys under the legal military age highlights the way that the war broke down differences between men and boys and challenged conventional middle-class views of childhood and youth. Most Northern boys did not become drummers or soldiers, but the fact that thousands did join the Union army challenged age-old assumptions about youth and maturity, flew in the face of the established but still developing notions of a nurtured, protected childhood, and showed an extreme version of the divergent ways that boys and girls were expected to participate in the war effort. While boys were allowed—in fiction and in real life—to risk their lives for their country and to transcend the normal boundaries of childhood, acceptable roles for girls in the war simply reflected the domestic responsibilities they would assume in a few years as wives and mothers.

Perhaps Northerners associated drummer boys—at least the ones who suffered injury and death in the service of their country—with the dead and dying children who had been featured in some children's magazines years before the war began. For example, the denominational magazine *Youth's Companion* filled its columns with obituaries and stories of youngsters accepting Jesus on their deathbeds. During the Civil War, *The Little Pilgrim* still featured occasional articles, often sent in by grieving parents, about the death of young readers. These articles were supposed to inspire readers to live better lives, to think about their lives after death, to take their religion seriously. By making these young victims into models of piety, poems and stories and letters such as these made children's deaths serve a purpose: if it taught other children to be better persons, the death of even the youngest child was not wasted. In the same way the "dead drummer boys"—and the living ones too—who filled magazines and newspapers during the Civil War were models for Americans of all ages, for if young boys could demonstrate patriotism and courage, adults certainly could too.

The stories and books that painted quite upbeat portraits of drummer boys giving the ultimate sacrifice drew heavily on the spiritual ramifications of their deaths. While acknowledging the tragedy of the untimely deaths of these brave boys and presenting heartfelt scenes of tearful funerals and mourning friends and families, authors concentrated much more on the wonderful examples the "dead drummer boys" had provided for their older but less wise and less noble elders. As long as the story concerned the religious convictions of the drummers, or the positive ways these young soldiers could encourage the reform of their grizzled, sinful comrades, the Northern public apparently could accept the idea that very young boys were being placed in harm's way. The story of Clarence McKenzie, the "dutiful, beautiful" drummer for the Thirteenth New York, begins with his eager acceptance of an invitation to attend a neighborhood Sunday School some time before the onset of the war. His parents are not religious but are nevertheless kind; they allow Clarence and his sisters to attend the school, where they become the best-behaved and most pious children in the class. Clarence's later desire to join the army as a drummer is presented as part of a continuum, in a sense, of becoming an exemplar of all the personal and spiritual values that American children were supposed to embrace.[56]

Clarence died after being accidentally shot by a soldier cleaning his gun. The boy's biographer estimated that three thousand people attended his funeral in Brooklyn. "What brought out that vast throng of people? What led these thousands of people to pay their tribute of respect to this mere child? It was more than the mere occasion. It was more than the mere fact that he was a child of a regiment, and had met his death by such a mysterious providence. . . . There was a chord of tender sympathy deeper than all this. It was that mystical bond which binds the hearts of all God's children in one great brotherhood." Crowded into the funeral were his public school classmates, his Sunday School classmates, and hundreds of other mourners and supporters. The fiery funeral sermon linked Clarence's death with the Union cause: "This, he said, was among the first fruits of the rebellion; and it stood the country in hand to drive the traitors, who brought on this war, and who were the responsible authors of this child's death, down to the Gulf of Mexico, and crush the conspiracy forever." Later in the ceremony, the Bible that Clarence had been given by his minister, from which he had read one last chapter for his mother before leaving home, and which he had read every day in camp, was produced as a kind of relic linking faith with patriotism. Completing the image of the church militant in the face of treason, soldiers escorted his coffin to the cemetery and fired three rounds over the grave.[57]

Fearful Scenes

The militarization that affected virtually every Northern child was not for everyone. Only two when the war began, Ruth Huntington Sessions hated every warlike sound and bit of information that breeched the security of her Cambridge, Massachusetts, home. She could hear the "almost daily horror" of cannons firing on Boston Common and the bells tolling and the military bands playing the "dead march" at funerals. Household servants deepened her fears by gossiping about "wounds, and legs shot away and bullet holes in foreheads." Ruth was so frightened of war that, even when she heard the happier sounds of victory marches and parades, she retreated into a closet until the music faded away.[58]

An uncommon description of a young boy's reluctance to partake in military play appeared in the *Monthly Chronicle*, a handwritten newspaper published by a boy in Worcester, Massachusetts. Confronting the loss and grief spawned by the war, "The Little Soldier" surrenders the trumpet, gun, and sword that his mother had given him, explaining sadly, "I shall choose some other play." He explains,

> Mother! I have just been reading
> What a soldiers' life must be.
> And of fearful scenes of carnage
> He on battlefields must see.

Knowing how terrible war really was, he would give up his favorite pastime, dedicating his life instead to "labors . . . of love and mercy."[59]

But for every frightened little girl or boy there was a tough youngster who caught the spirit of the times. Ten-year-old Frank Rogers took so seriously his army surgeon father's parting instructions to care for his mother that he secretly carried around a loaded revolver to fend off any Copperheads who might threaten her. Thousands of boys did become drummers while tens of thousands more—and a few girls—imagined themselves as defenders of the Union and wished they could test their mettle in combat. But in their play, their reading, and their dreams, they were just as thoroughly, if safely, militarized.[60]

All Quiet Along the Potomac

🖋 THERE WERE MANY AFTERMATHS to the Civil War for Northern children.

Johnny Clem, the drummer boy–hero of Chickamauga, stayed in the army at the end of the war—he was still only fourteen years old—as a second lieutenant. By the time he retired from the army in 1916, he was a major general. Alexander Johnson, an African American who as a teenager had been one of the original drummer boys of the famous Fifty-fourth Massachusetts, suffered from chronic health problems after his Civil War service. Although he was active in the Grand Army of the Republic for many years and fathered seventeen children before his death at the age of eighty-three, he depended on a modest government pension to keep his family fed and sheltered.[1]

Children continued to play with war-inspired games—toy soldiers and guns had been in style for some time before the war too. But one of the more ambitious playthings produced after Appomattox, and the one that drew most directly on the war culture that had infused the North, was Milton Bradley's Myrioptican. Bradley had begun publishing greeting cards and small books during the war, but what made his company into a giant in the game industry was this miniature version of a panorama, complete with its own nonsensical but impressive-sounding name. The pictures that the "pro-

Is shot as he walks on his beat to and fro,
By a rifleman hid in the thicket."

But these small skirmishes and ambushes will not "count in the news
of the battle"; no officers are lost, just "a private or two now and
then." The action moves to an individual soldier, standing guard,
whose thoughts inevitably turn to his wife and young children.

His musket falls slack—his face dark and grim,
Grows gentle with memories tender,
And he mutters a prayer for the children asleep—
For their mother—may Heaven defend her.

He treads his weary path, distracted perhaps by images of home.
Then

Hark! Was it the night wind that rustled the leaves?
Was it moonlight so wondrously flashing?
It looked like a rifle—"Ha! Mary, good-bye!"
And the life-blood is ebbing and plashing.

But the sentry's death will hardly be noticed.

All quiet along the Potomac to-night,
No sound save the rush of the river;
While soft falls the dew on the race of the dead—
The picket's off duty forever.

Although not specifically an anti-war poem, "All Quiet Along the
Potomac" certainly humanizes the casualties that had risen to nearly
unfathomable numbers by the end of the war, suggests some of the
tensions raised by a society that still tended to shower respect on
elites at the expense of common soldiers, and highlights the strong
ties between home and battlefront.[3]

A sampling of the war's aftermaths suggests its direct and indi-
rect effects on a wide range of institutions and on the memories and
values of the Northern children who lived through it.

prietor" spooled through a cardboard box elaborately decorate
theater stage were colorful but rather crude renderings of doz
important events in the war, from the evacuation of Fort S
and the early-war martyrdom of Elmer Ellsworth to the bat
tween the *Monitor* and the *Virginia* and the Peninsula campa
the way through Grant at Vicksburg, Sherman's army on the
in Georgia, and the evacuation of Richmond. Along th
certain military details are displayed—not unusual in fu
wartime panoramas—including soldiers foraging for food
neers erecting telegraph lines under fire, a hospital, and Co
ate prisoners of war. The lucky children who received thi
pricey toy got everything they needed to put on their own
tion, from advertising posters and admission tickets to th
tious promotional material calling the Myrioptican "one
most interesting and instructive exhibitions that has ever b
sented to the public." More important was the seven-page
explaining the pictures. The instructions suggested that,
"some things may be said in a sportive way"—the scene
soldiers chasing down frightened pigs is called "pig-chew-r
"the historical statements and dates are intended to be a
accurate," and were repeated in appropriately solemn tone

For a time Northern children found reminders of th
their schoolbooks. A poem from a textbook published ju
after the Confederate surrender provided a faint echo of
conflict. "The Picket Guard" was an ironic, somber, and
tal poem, first published in 1861, that became a popular so
and after the war with its more popular title, drawn fror
line: "All quiet along the Potomac." The poem contrast
reports to headquarters of relative inaction along the un
occupied by the Union and Confederate armies.

"All quiet along the Potomac," they say;
"Except now and then a stray picket

Stern Stuff: Homecomings

Of course, most memoirists and diarists do not plan their writing based on the kinds of questions that historians reading their personal papers a century or more later might ask. One of the questions that would occur to almost anyone considering the lives of Civil War children is: what was it like when fathers came home from years away in the army, strangers to their children and wives, changed forever, perhaps, after the terrors they witnessed and the hardships they endured. But, unaware of the inquiring minds of posterity, few personal narratives written by men and women who were children during the war describe this dramatic moment beyond relatively generic expressions of relief and happiness.

Eliza Starbuck, who had been a young girl on Nantucket during the war, had only a single memory of her mother's nephew, the "Cousin Seth" whom she did not actually meet until after the war. She had known of him and had sensed his cocky, dashing, and "devil-may-care" attitude, only from a photograph taken of the young man upon his enlistment in the army. He wore his cap at a daring angle and had a twinkle in his eye as "he sat easily in his armchair with his knees crossed in a sort of nonchalance." But like so many other soldiers, Seth came home a changed man, scarred by long months in Richmond's Libby Prison. Seth had been a fine physical specimen when he left for the war, but the man who returned was not the boy Eliza had come to know from the photograph. "In that quiet voice which had the curious hint of finality that I've always noticed in the returned soldier," he described his experiences in prison, where a close friend had died in his arms. Prison had ravaged his body and broken his spirit; Eliza never saw him again, for he died shortly after returning home. Eliza wondered if, had he lived, "the twinkle would ever have come back to those deep-set gray eyes! Or was everything 'different'?"[4]

The most elaborate account of a father's homecoming came from the pen of short story writer Hamlin Garland. His father

Richard spent nearly two years fighting and marching with Sherman's men in the western theater, leaving behind a wife and three children—the oldest daughter, Hattie, five-year-old Hamlin, and two-year-old Frank. Garland spent the first few pages of his autobiography describing Richard's appearance on their hardscrabble farm in Wisconsin at the end of the war; he also wrote a much longer fictional version, from the point of view of the returning soldier, in "The Return of a Private." The latter begins with the private and a few comrades getting off a train. The townsfolk are too used to soldiers coming home to pay much attention to these dusty, tired veterans. The men sleep a little but are anxious to get home, so they set out on foot.

The scene turns to the private's family, who know that their husband and father survived the war but are not quite sure when he will arrive. They are visiting a neighbor's house—within eyeshot of their little farm—when they spot a gaunt stranger trudging wearily up to their gate. Emma, the wife, suddenly recognizes her husband Edward, gathers her children—an older girl and two boys about the same age as Hamlin and his brother in 1865—and dashes for home. Meanwhile the veteran "was like a man lost in a dream. His wide, hungry eyes devoured the scene. The rough lawn, the little unpainted house, the field of clear yellow wheat behind it, down across which streamed the sun." He cannot get enough of it: "How peaceful it all was. . . . How far removed from all camps, hospitals, battle lines." It was humble but "majestic in its peace. How did he ever leave it for those years of tramping, thirsting, killing?"

Then his wife is upon him, breaking his reverie, embracing and kissing him as the children stand in "a curious row," daughter sobbing, sons uncertain. The veteran hugs Mary, the girl, then turns to the little boys. Tommy, the older one, greets him, but little Teddy hangs back, peering at his father from behind the fence. "Come here, my little man; don't you know me?" The awkward moment veers toward disappointment. "The baby seemed like some other woman's child, and not the infant he had left in his wife's arms." The war had come between him and his baby—he was only a strange man to him. Eventually the soldier offers Teddy an apple and, pushed and encouraged by his big brother, the little boy finally succumbs and "a moment later was kicking and squalling in his father's arms."

They go inside, the veteran stretches out on the floor, taking off his shoes, relaxing with a pillow, enjoying his status as "a free man again, no longer a soldier under command." He talks almost non-stop, asking questions about the farm and neighbors, telling of his aches and pains and fevers, mourning the favored dog who had died during his absence, and relishing Emma's biscuits, which he had bragged about so often. He shows them scars from the wounds that had nearly left them fatherless and widowed. It was a magical moment, only slightly marred by the hard work that lay ahead: "His farm was weedy and encumbered . . . his children needed clothing, the years were coming upon him, he was sick and emaciated, but his heroic soul did not quail. With the same courage with which he had faced his Southern march he entered upon a still more hazardous future."

The story ends happily—at least the day ends happily in the story—with little Teddy falling asleep in his father's arms. But Hamlin placed a kind of coda on the tale that broadened its meaning and offered a characteristically enigmatic assessment: "The common soldier of the American volunteer army had returned. His war with the South was over, and his fight, his daily running fight with nature and against the injustice of his fellow-men, was begun again."[5]

Garland's autobiography continues the story beyond the homecoming and helps explain the tone of the fictionalized version's ending. Despite the family's joy at Richard's return, "all was not the same as before." Even as a boy, Hamlin perceived the bitterness that he must have instinctively learned from his mother, who had begged her husband not to enlist. But, wrote Hamlin as an adult, "he was of the stern stuff which makes patriots." "What sacrifice, what folly! Like thousands of others he deserted his wife and children for an abstraction, a mere sentiment." Garland admitted in his autobiography that his memory of the actual events of those war years was dim, but he held that "a large part of what I am is due to the impressions of these deeply passionate and poetic years." The children loved to hear their father tell stories from the war. Yet a harsh side of Richard Garland also emerged, "for my father brought back from his two years' campaigning . . . the temper and habit of a soldier." He resumed his dominant place in the family—a change of pace for Hamlin and his little brother Frank, especially, who remembered nothing of their lives before Richard went away and had grown accustomed to their mother's lighter touch. "We soon learned . . . that the soldier's promise of punishment was swift and precise in its fulfillment." "We knew he loved us," Garland wrote in words that could no doubt have been echoed by thousands of soldiers' children, "for he often took us to his knees of an evening and told us stories of marches and battles, or chanted war-songs for us." But "the moments of his tenderness were few," and the slightest misbehavior was corrected harshly and immediately.[6]

Homecomings like this occurred at thousands of doors and gateways, in untold numbers of yards and barns and streets. And, like the little boy representing Hamlin Garland, they would no doubt "never forget that figure, that face. It will always remain as something epic, that return of the private."[7]

A Lasting Peace

Northern schoolbooks had not been as consumed by the war as their Confederate counterparts, and postwar texts continued to downplay the war. An American history textbook by Thomas Wentworth Higginson, the Unitarian minister, abolitionist, and colonel of a black regiment, ended with U. S. Grant's presidency and spent only about 50 of its 330 pages on the sectional conflict and Civil War combined. Aside from a fairly positive portrayal of John Brown, disdainful descriptions of President James Buchanan's dithering during the secession crisis, and a reference to the widespread rumor that Jefferson Davis had been captured wearing women's clothing, Higginson's *Young Folks' History of the United States* presented a generally evenhanded account of the great schism between North and South. Although Northern war aims are emphasized and Reconstruction described in far more generous terms than Southerners would have appreciated, the history of the sectional conflict and war is not told from a particularly partisan point of view.

Toward the end of the book, as Higginson brings the war to a close and assesses its causes and impact, he offers his version of the conciliatory attitude that even in 1875 had begun to characterize at least some of the public discourse about the war, and which would come to dominate most Americans' thinking by the turn of the century. Of course, Higginson could not excuse any person who fought to uphold slavery. Yet, he reminded his young readers, the United States itself did not emancipate the slaves "until compelled to it by military necessity." The awful treatment of Union prisoners by Confederates and atrocities like the massacre of African-American soldiers at Fort Pillow were also inexcusable, "but these were, after all, the acts of a few; and the general feeling in both armies was, no doubt, that of sincere and manly opponents." Higginson developed this idea that both sides fought nobly and virtuously for what they believed in, and argued that even the efforts of Confederates, however ignoble their cause, can and should be admired. The war had proven "that the strength, courage, and patriotism of the American people, were still as great as in the period of the Revolution." Few families did not lose a son or brother or father, and "on both sides the self-devotion of the women at home equaled that of the soldiers in the field." In the armies, "each side learned to respect the courage and resources of the other, and to feel, that, if Americans were once re-united, no foreign power could ever endanger their liberties." Higginson borrowed his final words on the war from Abraham Lincoln's second inaugural address, which he quoted at length, emphasizing its wistful tolerance, its laying of guilt for the sin of slavery on both sections, and its hope for a "lasting peace among ourselves and with all nations." Years before the children of the Civil War and their children came to embrace this unifying interpretation of the war's importance, Higginson shared his vision of peace and national well-being with the Civil War generation.[8]

Just as Higginson tried to replace warlike thoughts with peaceful ones, the militarization of children's literature dwindled within a few years. Oliver Optic's trilogies about the Somers brothers completed their runs during the year after the fighting ended, while *Our Young Folks* published a series of articles in 1865 describing visits to Southern battlefields. A four-volume history of the war by Mary S. Robinson appeared between 1866 and 1871, telling the story of the war through the experiences, conversations, and letters of a Northern family, one of whom goes off to the Union army in the first volume. The series was called *A Household Story of the American Conflict*, which included *The Brother Soldiers* (1866), *Forward with the Flag* (1871), *The Great Battle Year* (1871), and *The Work of the Two Great Captains* (1871).

Appropriately enough, *The Little Corporal*—the most self-consciously militaristic juvenile magazine spawned by the war—pursued its interest in the military and political events of the war longer than any other magazine. An October 1865 article called its loyal readers " 'wide-awakes' of another sort than those who used to wear the funny capes and hats" before the war, a reference to the Republican marching clubs of the 1850s. A lead article celebrated the New Year of 1867 by crowing "The New Year promises glorious things for *The Little Corporal*. His army is already rallying for the new campaign. New recruits are coming in by the thousands, and the old soldiers are doing valiant service as recruiting officers. I trust that all the grand army of 1866 will re-enlist as 'veterans.'" The over-wrought rhetoric was simply reminding readers to renew their sub-scriptions! "Hark to the voice of *The Little Corporal*. He calls again for volunteers. He wants no cowards, no skulkers. . . . But all those who are willing for another year to battle for the right, the good and true—to help to purify and glorify, by true living and doing, our free and freedom loving America!" This drum roll for subscribers combines perfectly the values touted by antebellum magazines with the martial terminology and patriotic spirit inculcated by the war.[9]

Despite the martial fervor of *The Little Corporal*, references to the war quickly faded from children's magazines. Yet the war had played a part in the transition in children's literature from a nar-rowly didactic and religious tone to an approach in which interest-ing and even exciting stories became more important than pious parables. Old chestnuts like *Youth's Companion* continued to be published (although *The Little Pilgrim* succumbed just a few years after the war ended), the American Sunday School Union and other evangelical societies continued to produce morally didactic litera-ture, and new magazines like *The Children's Hour* (which appeared from 1867 to 1874) were throwbacks to the authoritarian, sentimen-talized, and overtly religious journals of the prewar period.[10]

But the rate of change from stories with deep meanings to tales of adventure and entertainment nevertheless accelerated. Perhaps children had simply grown out of the simpler, earlier genres. Little Maggie Campbell, who had delighted in singing the bloodthirsty "We'll Hang Jeff Davis on a Sour Apple Tree," grew up to be Mar-garet Deland, the writer, and she recalled reading Mrs. Sherwood's *Little Henry and His Bearer*, about a "horrid, saintly" British boy liv-ing in India who converts his family, servants, and bearer to Chris-tianity on his deathbed. A contemporary also recalled the Sunday School literature of his boyhood with little fondness. He wrote many years later that he had "not forgiven the authors who wrote those dismal Sunday-school books with blue paper covers," whose "especial talent seemed to be to make goodness appear offensive and to add a glamor of attractiveness to evil." It seemed to him that "good little simpering Jane, and Willie, the prig, would be welcome as playmates only by other 'blue-covered book' children." Even *The Little Pilgrim* dropped the practice of publishing the obituaries of pious young readers by the end of 1865, and as one historian of children's literature has argued, the contents of post–Civil War children's magazines revealed "an increasing lightness of spirit." *Our Young Folks*—which during its eight-year run immediately after the Civil War featured some of the best writing of all the postwar periodicals, with contributions from such authors as Louisa May Alcott, Harriet Beecher Stowe, Thomas Wentworth Higginson, and Henry Wadsworth Longfellow—was part of the transition. Never outrageous or sensationalistic, it was also more balanced, with gentle humor, satisfying entertainment, and unpretentious lessons.[11]

Oliver Optic's *Student and Schoolmate* had already broadened the content of juvenile magazines in the 1850s and 1860s with large doses of political opinion, war stories, patriotic songs, "dialogues," and declamation pieces. When in 1866 Optic left his editor's desk at *Student and Schoolmate*, he almost immediately began editing *Oliver Optic's Magazine*, which continued his wartime penchant for exciting and interesting stories and features. Responding to criticism by such writers as Louisa May Alcott of his livelier and less moralistic stories, Optic warned against forcing every element of children's reading to be educational. "Do not be afraid of excitement, so long as it is healthy," he wrote in 1874; "do not keep young minds always on the high pressure system of instruction." Such publications as *Demorest's Young America* followed Optic's advice with exciting tales, comedic pieces, and historical sketches. Magazines published later in the century, like the *Boys of New York: A Paper for Young Americans*, aped dime novels with stories of working-class boys who became heroes by narrowly averting disasters, went on fantastic adventures all over the world, and demonstrated the value of pluck, daring, and luck. Other features included popular songs, theatrical announcements, and sporting news. *Frank Leslie's Boy's and Girl's Weekly* produced, in its editor's words, "Healthy Fiction, Romantic Adventures, Parlor Amusements, Science Made Easy . . . Anecdotes illustrating character . . . Instances of modern progress" and games, magic tricks, and other "Fireside Amusements for Winter Evenings," along with a generous helping of violence and adventure. Later in the century, the *Tip Top Weekly* specialized in exciting sports-related stories for boys.[12]

A favorite children's magazine published over the last quarter of the nineteenth century was introduced in an article in its parent magazine, *Scribner's*, which declared that most so-called children's magazines were actually aimed at parents. They were burdened with "sermonizing," the "wearying spinning out of facts," and the "rattling of the dry bones of history." *St. Nicholas Magazine*, asserted its new editor, Mary Mapes Dodge, would be a "pleasure-ground" for its young readers, where children could enjoy "a brand-new, free life of their own for a little while, accepting acquaintances as they choose and turning their backs without ceremony on what does not concern them." To that end, *St. Nicholas* featured travel pieces, biographies, scientific and historical studies, and practical lessons on such topics as physical fitness, sports and games, and crafts. The magazine's fiction offered excitement—Thomas Nelson Page's "Two Little Confederates," for instance, or stories of young heroes of the Revolution and Civil War—as well as mild domestic tales offering simple, secular advice on being responsible, well-liked children. *St. Nicholas* survived until well into the 1930s.

Perhaps inspired by wartime exploits of tough, active youth like the Somers twins, postwar literary boys became lovable rogues who might, in a tight spot, reveal their good hearts, their responsibility, even their piety, but whose primary goal was to have fun and whose primary literary purpose was to entertain young readers. Although the boy characters in Horatio Alger's stories often ended up improving their station in life through hard work, perseverance, and timely aid from a kindly benefactor, they were also a pretty rough-and-tumble sort, the kind that the former Unitarian minister could observe at the Newsboys Lodging House where he spent much of his time. These street children take care of one another; Ragged Dick, perhaps his most famous creation, is self-reliant and tough—yet he takes the time to tell fairy tales to a frightened little boy he has rescued. Dick later saves a little rich boy from drowning and is rewarded by the grateful father with a job. Alger's work, if not preachy, was quite plain in its condemnation of drinking, smoking, and gambling, and he displayed a great confidence in education. One of the greatest rewards his boy-heroes can receive is to be sent to school by the wealthy businessmen for whom they do favors.[13]

Other boys created by children's authors carried less of a moral burden. Thomas Bailey Aldrich and others gloried in the exploits of "bad boys," yet most were actually merely mischievous, or, as Aldrich wrote about himself in his autobiographical *Story of a Bad Boy*, "I was an amiable, impulsive lad, blessed with fine digestive powers, and no hypocrite." Oddly enough, Gillian Avery has detected a small "bad boy" undercurrent in books for boys in the nineteenth century: a regular and rather alarming love of explosives, ranging from the 1821 manual *The Art of Making Fireworks* through Metta V. Victor's *A Bad Boy's Diary* (the bad boy in this case "throws firecrackers at horses, shoots the minister with his father's pistol, puts gunpowder in the chimney, burns down the town hall and finishes by blowing up the new railroad bridge"), all the way to George Peck's favorite character—known only as "the boy"—who with his friends blows up a pesky, nasty dog with dynamite![14]

Although they were not exactly published as "children's literature," dime novels attracted mainly men and boys and, as a result, can be considered the culmination of the transition in reading material from tedious sermonettes to breathless action. Dime novels evolved out of the "story papers" of the 1840s and 1850s—tabloid-sized weeklies like *Brother Jonathon*, the *New York Ledger*, *Beadle's Weekly*, and the *Fireside Companion*—that featured fare for the whole family, ranging from serialized adventure stories and romances to stories of the West and historical fiction. The dime-novel format—a weekly, fifty-to-a-hundred-page pamphlet measuring four-by-six inches and costing a nickel or a dime—first appeared in the 1840s, but it took the firm of Beadle and Adams to perfect the genre. By 1865 they had printed an astonishing four million books; some titles sold eighty thousand copies. Many competitors jumped into the market for sensationalized fiction in the 1860s, but Beadle and Adams remained the preeminent publisher of the cheap, exciting fare that adolescents and young men gobbled up by the millions. A repackaging of the dime novel, the "cheap libraries" that began appearing in the 1870s, were actually series in which story formats or even main characters continued to appear week after week.[15]

One boy of the 1860s and 1870s offered just the sort of testimonial to dime novels that worried parents feared. Long after Otis Skinner reached adulthood, he recalled a banging shutter in the big old, noisy, scary house in which he lived. His "habit of novel reading helped along his terror." He loved to be frightened by the novels put out by Beadle, with their "bright orange covers" that "had an odor all their own." They told "tales of assassins, Indians and specter skippers; narratives so gruesome that he dared not continue reading, nor yet did he dare to blow down the chimney of the unlawful midnight lamp, because then it's all dark and things can get you before you can dive under the bedclothes." Skinner "had a cache of these forbidden paper-covered volumes at the foot of an apple tree in the yard which he secretly visited from time to time"—the same apple tree under which he smoked his first cigarette.[16]

Walter Brooks found his favorite reading matter in *Frank Leslie's Boy's and Girl's Weekly*. Because his parents disapproved of the tales of "hair-breadth escapes from death and danger," the magazine had to be subscribed to by the coachman and then read aloud to him by Walter. "But how trying it was to the patience to always have the chapters end just as the Indian had raised his rifle to his shoulder, taken deliberate aim and fired, and the next chapter to open with something entirely irrelevant and commonplace. There was a whole week to wait before the Indian's bullet did or did not reach a vital spot!"[17]

Henry Cabot Lodge also consumed dime novels, but he remembered—many years later—that he did so mainly because "it was felt to be fine and manly and a little wicked to read, with dark precautions, these quite uninteresting but enticingly forbidden books." This scion of a proper Boston family preferred, he wrote, Scott, Cooper, Defoe, Dickens, and Poe; the dime novels "were sensational and extravagant, and being destitute of art or imagination were really dull." Most boys would disagree; indeed, most parents would have disagreed—at least about the dull part.[18]

Moralists and parents bitterly denounced sensationalized literature. Although Beadle and Adams produced series called "American Sixpenny Biographies" and "Men of the Times," not to mention booklets with patriotic speeches and songs, cheap fiction was the dominant form produced by this publishing house and its competitors. The tall tales of outlaws and lawmen of the Old West, Indians and frontiersmen, and of big-city detectives and boy gangs, filled with—for the nineteenth century—strong language, amoral motivations, and lurid violence, were a far cry from the wholesome stories still appearing in favorite juvenile magazines like *St. Nicholas*. As early as 1839 a Presbyterian minister named James Alexander complained that the cheap story papers, which gave "occupation to many a poor reader for the whole of Sunday," were "frequently taken up with just that kind of reading which is fitted to make a sound mind sick, and a feeble mind crazy." They consisted mainly of "Tales upon tales of love, of horror, of madness, and these often the effusions of the most unpractised and contemptible scribblers." Wartime publishers for children had jump-started this transition to

adventure-oriented writing, both in dime novels and in more legiti-
mate publications for young people.[19]

Of course there was no strict cutoff point in the transition from
one type of literature to another. Instead there was the constant addition of layers of different kinds of literature for children. Edward
Mitchell, who as an adult would become editor of the *New York
Sun*, recalled a huge range of reading material in his 1850s and 1860s
childhood, from strict Puritan tracts to an abridged edition of *The
Arabian Nights*; from hymn books to Dickens; from history—
a two-volume *History of the Jewish War* stuck out in his memory because of its "sumptuous martial and architectural engravings"—
to *Uncle Tom's Cabin*; from somber Sunday School papers to *Vanity
Fair, Putnam's Monthly*, and the cartoons in *Harper's*.[20]

As the Civil War faded from children's magazines, so too did the
positive and relatively open-minded portrayals of African Americans.
The African Methodist Episcopal Church's *Christian Recorder* continued to publish uplifting and stern stories and articles for black children, but from time to time it featured a request from an African
American seeking information about parents, children, or other relatives who still lived in the South. As slaves, writers for magazines
published for white children seemed to think, African Americans
were interesting and sympathetic. As free people, however, they were
nearly invisible. In the 1870s *St. Nicholas* published mildly racist dog-
gerel that included parodies of "Little Miss Muffet," substituting eth-
nic stereotypes for the familiar young English girl. One was "Little
Peeky-Wang-Fu, with her chopsticks so new," who "sat eating her
luncheon of rice, When a rat running by, On the rice cast his eye,
And Peeky ran off in a trice." Other rhymes were put to the tune of a
popular minstrel song, "Zip Coon," while readers wrote enthusiastic
letters nattering on comfortably about "darky dolls" and "darky" advertising cards. *Our Young Folks*, a decidedly middle-class Yankee
journal with liberal leanings, nevertheless offered distracting phonetic
spellings of supposed African-American dialects and stereotypical

black characters who veered from the saintly to the roguish—but rarely in between.[21]

One Pittsburgh girl grew up having nightmares about a disturbingly racist image from a Sunday School paper, which featured a picture of a "lady in a white dress, with no hoopskirt on, but with a towel wrapped around her head, throwing a baby into a river— where a crocodile, with an open mouth full of sharp teeth, was waiting for it!" An accompanying song went, "See the heathen mother stand / Where the sacred current flows; / With her own maternal hand / 'Mid the waves her babe she throws. / Hark I hear the piteous scream; / Frightful monsters seize their prey, / Or the dark and bloody stream / Bears the struggling child away. / Send, oh send the Bible there . . ." The stereotypes and racism presented in children's literature during the last third of the nineteenth century simply reflected the racial assumptions of the larger society. Although the Civil War may have contributed to the broadening of topics and tones acceptable in children's literature, it could not permanently alter the racial notions that had lurked in writing for children for many years.[22]

A Pure and Holy Work

One wartime issue that would not—could not—go away after the shooting stopped was what to do with soldiers' orphans. A few small-scale efforts emerged during the last two years of the war, but the Soldiers' Orphans' Home movement quickly accelerated after Appomattox. Pennsylvania, Illinois, Kansas, Minnesota, Indiana, Iowa, Wisconsin, Rhode Island, Connecticut, and New Jersey all established state-supported institutions in the years immediately after the war. Some began as small private schools or homes that state governments eventually took over. Others became the pet projects of Republican politicians and veterans organizations. Orphans in

Indiana originally lived in the state-sponsored home for disabled veterans, until there were more orphans than veterans and a separate institution was established in 1870. A grant from the Camden and Amboy Railroad provided much of the seed money for the New Jersey home.[23]

As large, tax-supported institutions established during a time when Americans were unaccustomed and generally uncomfortable with such things, the soldiers' orphans' homes and schools foreshadowed later government programs. But they were also fat targets for penny-pinching Democrats, who after winning control of state legislatures in the late 1860s and 1870s sometimes closed the orphans' homes. Others worried about the potential for abuse and mistreatment of the children. The New Jersey Soldiers' Children's Home survived an 1872 investigation of reports of misbehavior by children and of inadequate care, but the home closed four years later. As early as 1874 the superintendent of the Illinois home could say that after surviving "investigation after investigation," her staff could continue their "pure and holy . . . work." Yet the accusations of harsh treatment and poor management continued throughout the long history of the home. The privately owned, profit-driven Pennsylvania system of orphans' schools was ripe for a wide array of abuses. After a newspaper charged the school administrators with profiteering, a critical state investigation and the withdrawal of support by the Grand Army of the Republic (GAR) led to the closing of most of the Pennsylvania schools by 1892.[24]

Even the most famous orphans' home sank into oblivion due to corruption and abuse. The National Homestead in Gettysburg grew from a nationwide campaign to locate the children of a dead soldier found clutching a photograph of two little boys and a girl. Sentimental Northerners appreciated the symbolism of these "Children of the Battlefield," who came to represent the thousands of sons and daughters who had lost their fathers in the cruel war. Newspapers and magazines around the country carried the story and the photo, and by November 1863 the widow and three children of Sgt. Amos Humiston had been located.

Northerners bought thousands of prints of the photograph and copies of a song based on the story. The composer of the song dedicated his royalties to "the support and education of the Orphan Children." Soon a campaign to establish a national orphanage for soldiers' orphans, promoted by Sunday Schools around the country, was under way. By 1866 the former Gettysburg headquarters of Maj. Gen. O. O. Howard, Humiston's commanding general, had been purchased and nearly two dozen children, including the Humistons (whose mother worked at the Homestead), were living there. For nearly a decade the National Homestead provided homes for as many as six dozen children. Yet the story of the orphans' refuge literally on the site of the bloodiest battle of the war ended with an ugly scandal when the matron and several members of her staff were convicted, fined, and thrown out of town in the mid-1870s for financial chicanery and mistreating the children. Despite a waiting list of orphans needing homes, it closed in the fall of 1877.[25]

Although the scale of the effort to care for war orphans dwarfed antebellum child-saving efforts and shifted most of the responsibility from individuals and private citizens to publicly supported institutions, many of the assumptions about the kinds of lives these children should lead remained the same. Like the orphanages, asylums, and refuges that predated them, the soldiers' orphans' homes were meant not only to provide for these deserving children of the country's patriotic martyrs but also to bring them up to be responsible, patriotic citizens. In most homes the children invested in their own maintenance by doing chores and working in home shops, and boys at many of the schools and homes were formed into military companies and drilled at least once a week. The "Home Cadets" at the Ohio Soldiers' and Sailors' Orphan Home consisted of the oldest and most physically fit boys (and, after 1887, girls), who drilled, formed a drum corps, and received training in tactics and the use of rifles.[26]

Frank Leslie's version of Amos Humiston clutching his children's photograph to his chest as he dies. *(Frank Leslie's Illustrated Newspaper, January 2, 1864. Courtesy of Mark Dunkelman)*

In the decades following the end of the war, soldiers' orphans reminded Americans of their duty to the men who had given their all for the Union. Continuing an antebellum practice, soldiers' orphans' schools often opened year-end examinations to the public, who could see that their tax dollars were creating well-educated and orderly citizens. Orphans also played central roles in ceremonies and events commemorating the war. At the first Memorial Day at Arlington National Cemetery in 1868, orphans of Union soldiers spread flowers over twelve thousand graves. On Decoration Day, children from the Gettysburg National Homestead traditionally strewed flowers on the graves at the National Cemetery while chanting an ode beginning "Lightly, lightly, lovingly tread / O'er the dust of the patriot dead." Pennsylvania orphans also appeared

The Humiston children appear on the cover of this sheet music of the song dedicated to them. *(Philadelphia: Lee & Walker, 1864. Courtesy of Mary Ruth Collins)*

when battle flags went on display and at gubernatorial inaugurations. Students at the New Jersey school "brought tears to eyes unused to weep," wrote their administrator, when they performed at an Independence Day flag-raising. Drill teams and bands from other homes participated in GAR encampments and in dedication ceremonies for war monuments.[27]

Most of the state homes for soldiers' orphans were strictly segregated, and relatively few children of African-American soldiers found beds in government-sponsored institutions. One of the few homes built expressly for African-American orphans, the Shelter for Orphans of Colored Soldiers and Friendless Colored Children in Baltimore, had the resources to provide for only about a dozen children at a time. The Brooklyn Colored Orphan Asylum, founded in 1866, focused on youngsters uprooted by the collapse of slavery rather than soldiers' orphans.[28]

Liberty Schools

The participation of schools in the home-front war effort helped cement the connection between education and patriotism. The function of using schools to promote peculiarly "American" values expanded after the war. But the process took on a more strident tone, as schools became symbols of the struggle to "Americanize" the immigrants pouring into the United States as well as the Native Americans whose conquest the U.S. army was finally completing in the 1870s and 1880s. The Republican weekly magazine *Judge* portrayed a beneficent Uncle Sam dragging a little Indian boy in headband and loincloth toward Miss Columbia's "Liberty School," where he would join the Chinese and African-American children waiting for him at the door. The schoolhouse was also employed as a symbol in racist attacks on immigrants and Catholicism by such artists as Thomas Nast, who once portrayed mitered Catholic priests as crocodiles attacking a valiant public school teacher and students. Later, anti-immigrant organizations like the American Protective Association and the Ku Klux Klan included pictures of schoolhouses on the mastheads of their official publications.[29]

Even when they were not accompanied by such blatant anti-immigrant attitudes, the efforts to acculturate the children of Native Americans and immigrants were rarely subtle. Policymakers insisted that the immigrants be rebuilt from scratch: they had to be taught cleanliness and diligence, basic reading, writing, and math skills, and, perhaps more important, how to be "American." Like decades earlier, when schools were supposed to shape boys into "young republicans" and wartime children into patriots, the urban schools overflowing with immigrants were supposed to season traditional school with lessons on loyalty and morality for new Americans. The influx of southern and eastern Europeans late in the century, and the perception among community leaders and educators that they posed a possible threat to order and progress, inspired local and state governments to step up their educational programs in the 1890s. In New York City, more schools were built (some classrooms in immigrant neighborhoods had been crammed with one hundred students), the school bureaucracy was professionalized and centralized, a pilot school lunch program was introduced, and between 1903 and 1913 the age for mandatory school attendance was raised from twelve to sixteen (though it was erratically enforced). Schools in many other cities took similar steps to "Americanize" immigrant children.[30]

Thousands of miles to the west, the U.S. military took advantage of peace between the North and South to finish the job it had begun before the war of corralling Native Americans on reservations, bringing thousands of other children into the sphere of government influence. In the 1870s, when the final campaigns against the unconquered tribes of the Plains and the Southwest began, Congress increased appropriations to religious schools. By the late 1870s federally administered day and boarding schools had begun to appear on reservations throughout the West. At the same time a new generation of "reformers" began calling for a major effort to assimilate Indians into the American mainstream. The notion that Native Americans could one day be "civilized" had a long history in the United States, but most efforts to accomplish it depended vaguely on restricting Indians to reservations and forcing them to become farmers and ranchers. Even the schools set up by religious organizations and the federal government remained fairly close to the reservations assigned to various tribes.

Richard Henry Pratt, a career army officer, changed all this by suggesting that young Native Americans would never become completely assimilated unless they were removed from the influence of older generations and taught useful trades. In 1878 he managed to get seventeen male youth admitted to the famous African-American Hampton Institute in Norfolk, Virginia. There he introduced the quartet of emphases that would characterize Indian education for decades: the English language, the work ethic, Christian values, and productive citizenship. By inculcating these values and assumptions, Pratt would "civilize" and "Americanize" the American Indian. He later went on to found the most famous school for Indians at Carlisle Barracks, Pennsylvania, where he created the model nonreservation boarding school. Far removed from their native environment, where tradition and backwardness dragged them down, Indian children would be changed into model Americans through academic discipline, hard work through manual training, and moral guidance.

Pratt's ideas quickly caught the imagination of other reformers anxious to find a way to improve the lives of the nation's "wards," as Native Americans were called. Although not all shared Pratt's confidence that Indians would one day be the equal of whites in skill and intelligence—even the most sympathetic educators tended to relegate Native American students to an inferior place in society—they did adopt his beliefs that the only way to guarantee the effectiveness of the new lessons was to remove students from their families and eliminate their heritage.

Indian boarding schools lasted well into the twentieth century, though the results of force-feeding "American" values and habits to Native American children were mixed. On the other hand, most children of immigrants eagerly embraced the ways of the new world—though tensions often arose between them and parents who insisted on retaining at least some of their traditional ways and beliefs. The association of schools with patriotism and the expansion of their role as agents of socialization during the Civil War found even greater application during the decades following the end of the conflict. Throughout the twentieth century, schools would be mobilized to support war efforts.

A Struggle So Momentous Ought to Have Some Value

Civil War children took their own lessons away from the war. Like the generations who grew up during the Great Depression or World War II or the 1960s, childhood experiences shaped later adult assumptions and attitudes in sometimes dramatic ways. The long-term effects of having lived through the Civil War could be rather startling. Take the case of Theodore Roosevelt. Since he was a boy of three when the war began, he could no doubt barely remember most of the events of the war that cast a long shadow over his adult attitudes and beliefs. Roosevelt's commitment to the "strenuous life" was well known during his lifetime, as was his somewhat more mythic policy of walking softly and carrying a big stick. Taking these notions to their logical but rather extreme conclusion, "no other prominent American of his day," according to one historian, "spent so much time thinking and writing about the meaning of war . . . with such deep emotional fervor." Roosevelt's wartime experiences consisted mainly of watching parades from the balcony of his parents' posh New York home, sporting his own Zouave uniform, and eagerly listening to stories about the adventures of his blockade-running uncles on his mother's side (and creating a game he called "Running the Blockade," which he and his sister played in Central Park). His father, a prominent businessman and political insider, had hired a substitute to serve in the army in his place, a decision that family members believed to have disappointed and even shamed the adult T. R. (It should be noted that the father was absent from home for nearly two years serving on a government commission managing soldiers' pay allotments to their families.)

Roosevelt's childhood excitement about the war and his adult dismay that his father had not played a military role in it, combined with his postwar acquaintanceship with generals like U. S. Grant and William T. Sherman and Lincoln's aide John Hay, created an obsession with the Civil War. It was, he might have said, the original "good war"; it settled a long-standing and worsening sectional strife, brought out the best in the brave men who fought to save the Union, and strengthened the United States and raised its influence in the world. Upholding the Constitution and the Union was an eminently just cause, and the feats of valor displayed by the fighting men on both sides were worthy exemplars of the masculine ideal.

All these positive impressions of the glory and efficacy and honor of war caused Roosevelt to pine for his own chance on the battlefield. From time to time he wondered if the country might not "need" to fight a war, to toughen up its flabby youth and purify its national conscience. His adolescent fight against asthma and a warning he received about a heart condition as a young newlywed led him to make a soldierly commitment to exercise and to exhibit physical courage whenever he could. He climbed the Matterhorn after learning he had a heart condition. He jumped at the chance to lead his "Rough Riders" against the Spanish—"his one day in battle," claims a biographer, "meant more to him than all his years in the White House," though he later regretted not receiving a disfiguring wound as a permanent commemoration of his courage and sacrifice—and bitterly resented not being allowed to lead troops during World War I. He conducted his political campaigns like military operations. In 1912 he nearly received the wound he had sought fifteen years before when a would-be assassin shot him in the chest on his way to give a speech in Milwaukee. Bleeding but undaunted, Roosevelt made the appearance anyway—ever the good soldier.[31]

Theodore Roosevelt was a complex, creative, and extremely intelligent man, and it would be inaccurate to attribute all of his martial enthusiasm to his boyhood experiences during the Civil War. Yet the war did contribute in some obvious and not so obvious ways to the development of ideas and attitudes that were exhibited throughout his adult life and his political career.

At least one Civil War child thought long and hard, as an adult, about what the Civil War meant to him. Henry Cabot Lodge's autobiography dealt in great detail with those elements of the war that a privileged member of the Boston elite had experienced. Yet he separated his war memories from the chronological account of his life. "I could not in the last chapter," he wrote, "say anything of the terrible ordeal through which the country was passing during my first four years at Mr. Dixwell's school. It was too great and too solemn to be mixed up with random memories of boyish sports and school experiences."[32]

Ever aware of his family's Federalist and Whig background, Lodge had, at his father's urging, "hollered for Fremont" in 1856 and worn a Lincoln badge in 1860. But despite the occasional visits to the Lodge home of such Republican luminaries as Charles Sumner, the great military events of the war overshadowed the boy's interest in politics. Too young to fight, Lodge nevertheless remembered himself as a great patriot who lashed out at "our Democratic Irish groom" when he suggested that Sherman would never reach the sea, and who took pride that the officer who halted the Boston draft riot with a blast of grapeshot was a relative. His daily life was dominated by the war. "You saw it in the streets," he wrote, "in the early makeshifts for money, in the paper currency, in the passing soldiers, in the neighboring camps." He watched Governor John Andrew send regiments off to war in 1861 and Robert Gould Shaw's Fifty-fourth Massachusetts march out of town two years later, and drilled with his school's military company. At theaters "every sentence which could be twisted into a patriotic allusion was loudly cheered." He and his friends attended Sanitary Fairs, wore military caps, and worried over absent relatives and friends. "This reading the death-roll and scanning bulletins to see how many men whom you have known and cared for, whose people are your people and whose fate is dear to you, have been killed is not an experience that one ever forgets." He recalled a Sunday when news of a great defeat of the Union armies arrived in Boston; the churches stayed open after morning services so congregants could gather to roll bandages and prepare lint to send to the army.[33]

But these memories were only the superficial remnants of the dramatic events he witnessed. Even though he had been only ten when the war began, and though his home was never in danger from the enemy, "it has seemed to me that the impressions of a boy . . . are not without importance, because everything which may serve to explain or characterize or illustrate a struggle so momentous ought to have some value to those of the future who would seek the truth about the past." Lodge believed that his entire generation probably had a different set of attitudes than Americans born after the war ended. "The feeling about the country of those to whom the Civil War is not mere history, but a living memory, is, I am certain, a little different from that of any others." Having witnessed their "country . . . at death grips with a destroying antagonist, reeling on the edge of the abyss," they came to appreciate its value and to know the cost of sustaining it. Those men "who lived through the war times have a more tender sentiment about their country . . . are more easily moved by all that appeals to their sense of patriotism, and . . . are less dispassionate no doubt in judging America and the American people than others."[34]

An event that occurred just after Congress declared war on Spain in 1898 made a huge impression on Lodge: a regiment called the Sixth Massachusetts was once again sent to Washington and once again had to pass through Baltimore. Rather than simply changing trains at the station—which the earlier incarnation of the regiment could not have done and is why they had to march through the city in the first place—the figurative sons and grandsons of the Civil War version of the regiment chose to march through the city to the other station once again. This time, rather than bricks and boos, crowds threw flowers and cheers their way. Lodge, who as a senator favored the war with Spain, walked with the regiment for the entire route and left with the conviction that the Northern men who had died during the riot and the war "had not died in vain," and that the unity of the country in supporting the Spanish conflict "demonstrated once for all this great fact."[35]

But the Civil War left Lodge with several more substantive "profound convictions which nothing can ever shake." First, his knowledge of the war made him optimistic about the future of the United States. Despite the problems caused by industrialization, the centralization of wealth, and immigration in the decades after the Civil War, knowing that "the nation came through the most terrible ordeal which any nation can undergo" convinced Lodge that the American people could meet any crisis. Second, he naturally admired the heroes of the Northern war effort while at the same time acknowledging Southerners' right "to glorify all they did and to exalt their own heroes." Yet he decried the fashion among Northerners, two generations after the war, to accept uncritically the Southern side of the war and implicitly or explicitly reject the values and ideas that had fueled Northern patriotism. "We should think ill of the Southern people if they did not" cherish their own institutions and patriots, but "that which is most praiseworthy in Southerners is discreditable in a Northerner." Lodge had learned from the war the importance of committed patriotism. "I can understand and I profoundly admire the man who was loyal to the nation against his State. I can understand the man who was loyal to his State against the nation." But the war had nurtured in him a distrust of "men who were loyal neither to their State nor to their nation." Men who were "loyal to nothing . . . risked nothing" and were, in fact, worse than the most determined Rebels. Another "lesson" Lodge took away from the war was "the hostility which I imbibed against England," due particularly to the "exquisite stupidity" displayed by its government in dealing with the United States during the war. He recalled the "impotent rage" he would feel whenever he read misguided editorials in English newspapers. His hatred was later replaced by a contempt that would influence his opposition to the proposed League of Nations after World War I. Lodge admitted that he had never "felt the slightest deference to English opinion."[36]

Finally, Lodge declared in his memoir that these "truisms" had been "pushed aside" recently "as if they were something to be ashamed of, as if they might be true but were certainly disagreeable and might possibly hurt somebody's feelings." He knew, and he wanted all Americans to understand, that "there was a right and a wrong in the Civil War." Slavery was wrong. Southerners may have been courageous and principled, but they had been absolutely wrong in trying to break up the United States on behalf of "a crime against humanity." Those in the North who "try to pretend that both sides were right" ignored history and the truth. "Events have shown inexorably that it was the right which triumphed at Appomattox." This was what the war meant to one old man who had carried "the faiths of my boyhood born in the war time" through his long and distinguished career as a politician and public servant.[37]

A quite different set of memories emerged from the wartime experiences of Anna Howard Shaw, who as an adult would become a pioneering Methodist minister, doctor, and advocate for women's suffrage (she served as president of the National Women's Suffrage Movement for more than a decade). Not surprisingly, her memoir concentrated more on the plight of the women and children left behind than on the political and military events of the period. She remembered the period very differently from Roosevelt and Lodge, and though her war was hardly representative of all Northern girls', her memoir suggests that they may have felt left out of the great events of the war.

Born in England in 1847, Shaw was raised in New England, where her father provided for his growing family as a laborer and craftsman but also took part in many liberal causes, including abolitionism. Their happy existence in the civilized East was shattered when her father got it in his head to move to the frontier with a group of other Englishmen. "None of these men had the least practical knowledge of farming," Shaw later wrote with a trace of contempt. The cluelessness of her father—and of men in general—was a theme in Anna's memoir. Shaw was twelve when the family moved to the wilderness, a hundred miles from the railroad terminus in Grand Rapids, Michigan. On an earlier visit, her father had built a crude cabin for them, but he left them with no furniture and uncleared fields before returning to his old job in Massachusetts. He stayed there for two years; his family—an older brother and two sisters, Anna, a younger brother, and her mother—was left to fend for itself. When they arrived at the ramshackle dwelling, "forty miles from the nearest post-office, and half a dozen miles from any neighbors save Indians, wolves, and wildcats," "wholly unlearned in the ways of the woods as well as in the most primitive methods of farming," Shaw's mother sank to the ground. "We stood around her in a frightened group, talking to one another in whispers. Our little world had crumbled under our feet."

The next two years were trying, and Shaw clearly blamed her father, who, "like most men . . . should never have married." He worked away in Lawrence, sending small sums of money irregularly, but "a generous supply of improving literature for our minds" quite regularly. Struggling to carve out a farm in the virgin forest of northern Michigan, the family confronted "the relentless limitations of pioneer life . . . on every side, and at every hour of the day." Her father finally joined them—just in time for the beginning of the war. By mid-1862 two brothers and her father had joined the army. At the age of fifteen Shaw was "the principal support of our family, and life became a strenuous and tragic affair." She taught school and helped her mother do sewing and washing; they also took in boarders. A sister married, gave birth to a child, and died; the baby, the sole bright point in their sad lives, was eventually taken away when his father remarried. Life "grew harder with every day." It was "an incessant struggle to keep our land, to pay our taxes, and to live." Her health began to fail as she walked several miles to and from the country school where she taught every day.

"These were years I do not like to look back upon," Shaw wrote fifty years later. They were "years in which life had degenerated into a treadmill whose monotony was broken only by the grim messages from the front." After Appomattox the men returned home and the pressure lifted. She was eighteen, and "the end of the Civil War brought freedom to me, too." She began saving some of her money for college. When she finally left for Albion College, she never looked back. Anna Howard Shaw's bitter memoir serves as a reminder that "normal" life did not halt while the Civil War raged. It also provides stark evidence of the drastic effects that the absence of men from the home front could have on the women and children left behind. The war was not a glorious, patriotic episode in every child's life; for many, the war was simply another burden in already difficult lives.[38]

As in so many aspects of American life, the Civil War exerted a powerful influence on Northern children, their families, and on the institutions that shaped both. Some of those effects were immediate and material, as fathers failed to come home, as family fortunes were ruined, or as members of families came to appreciate one another even more than they had before the war. Some effects surfaced in changing or broadening assumptions about the functions of government and books in children's lives, while others emerged only after Civil War children became adults, when their war experiences were reflected in their careers and political choices and assumptions about how the world operated. "The War Spirit at Home" referred to specific ideas and assumptions during the war, but for many children that spirit was extended far into their lives, refracted and altered, to be sure, but as monuments to the lives of Northern children during the Civil War.

Notes

Introduction: A Struggle Touching All Life

1. James Oliver Horton and Lois E. Horton, *Black Bostonians: Family Life and Community Struggle in the Antebellum North,* rev. ed. (New York: Holmes and Meier, 1999), 2–3; Leon F. Litwack, *North of Slavery: The Negro in the Free States, 1790–1860* (Chicago: University of Chicago Press, 1961), 153–186, 235–237; David M. Katzman, *Before the Ghetto: Black Detroit in the Nineteenth Century* (Urbana: University of Illinois Press, 1973), 23–27; Robert J. Cottrell, *The Afro-Yankees: Providence's Black Community in the Antebellum Era* (Westport, Conn.: Greenwood, 1982), 114; Graham Russell Hodges, *Slavery and Freedom in the Rural North: African Americans in Monmouth County, New Jersey, 1665–1865* (Madison, Wisc.: Madison House, 1997), esp. 174–178, 188–195.
2. Hermon W. DeLong, Sr., *Boyhood Reminiscences,* comp. by William D. Conklin (Dansville, N.Y.: Dansville Press, 1982), 70–73.
3. Ruth Huntington Sessions, *Sixty-Odd: A Personal History* (Brattleboro, Vt.: Stephen Daye, 1936), 31; Bureau of the Census, *Historical Statistics of the United States: Colonial Times to 1970,* Pt. 1 (Washington, D.C.: Government Printing Office, 1975), 23.

Chapter 1. Childhood in Antebellum America

1. DeLong, *Boyhood Reminiscences,* 75.
2. John Quincy Adams, *An Old Boy Remembers* (Boston: Ruth Hill, 1935), 18–20; Otto Kallir, ed., *Grandma Moses: My Life's History* (New York: Harper and Brothers, 1948), 21–22, 26; Robert Dudley, *In My Youth* (Indianapolis: Bobbs-Merrill, 1914), 209.
3. Eric F. Goldman, ed., "Young John Bach McMaster: A Boyhood in New York City," *New York History* 20 (1939), 320–321.

4. DeLong, *Boyhood Reminiscences*, 77.

5. David Wallace Adams and Victor Edmonds, "Making Your Move: The Educational Significance of the American Board Game, 1832 to 1904," *History of Education Quarterly* 17 (Winter 1977), 370–373; Robert K. Weis, "To Please and Instruct the Children," *Essex Institute Historical Collections* 123 (1987), 117–149, Child quote on 124; Walter Brooks, *A Child and a Boy* (New York: Brentano's, 1915), 44–45.

6. Jeannette L. Gilder, *The Autobiography of a Tomboy* (New York: Doubleday, Page and Co., 1900), 6–8.

7. Alice E. Kingsbury, *In Old Waterbury* (Waterbury, Conn.: Mattatuck Historical Society, 1942), n.p.; Eleanor Hallowell Abbott, *Being Little in Cambridge When Everyone Else Was Big* (New York: D. Appleton-Century Co., 1936), 138–141; Margaret Deland, *If This Be I, As I Suppose It Be* (New York: D. Appleton-Century Co., 1936), 141.

8. Daniel Beard, *Hardly a Man Is Now Alive: The Autobiography of Dan Beard* (New York: Doubleday, Doran and Co., 1939), 104; Dudley, *In My Youth*, 25–35, 121, 205–206.

9. Carolyn L. Karcher, "Lydia Maria Child and the Juvenile Miscellany: The Creation of an American Children's Literature," in Kenneth M. Price and Susan Belasco Smith, eds., *Periodical Literature in Nineteenth-Century America* (Charlottesville: University Press of Virginia, 1995), 90–91.

10. Gillian Avery, *Behold the Child: American Children and Their Books, 1621–1922* (Baltimore: Johns Hopkins University Press, 1994), 146.

11. A wonderful encyclopedia of brief descriptions and basic facts about hundreds of children's magazines is R. Gordon Kelly, *Children's Periodicals of the United States* (Westport, Conn.: Greenwood Press, 1984).

12. Anne Scott MacLeod, *American Childhood: Essays on Children's Literature of the Nineteenth and Twentieth Centuries* (Athens: University of Georgia Press, 1994), 89.

13. *The Anti-Slavery Alphabet* (Philadelphia: Merrihow and Thompson, 1847), n.p.

14. Anne M. Boylan, *Sunday School: The Formation of an American Institution, 1790–1880* (New Haven: Yale University Press, 1988), 80–85; Chanta M. Haywood, "Constructing Childhood: The *Christian Recorder* and Literature for Black Children, 1854–1865," *African American Review* 36 (Fall 2002), 417–428.

15. Karcher, "Lydia Maria Child and the Juvenile Miscellany," 107–108; Donna C. MacCann, "The White Supremacy Myth in Juvenile Books About Blacks, 1830–1900" (Ph.D. dissertation, University of Iowa, 1988), 48–125.

16. Patricia C. Click, *The Spirit of the Times: Amusements in Nineteenth-Century Baltimore, Norfolk, and Richmond* (Charlottesville: University Press of Virginia, 1989), 22–25.

17. Otis Skinner, *Footlights and Spotlights: Recollections of My Life on the Stage* (New York: Blue Ribbon Books, 1923), 13–15.

18. Edward P. Mitchell, *Memoirs of an Editor: Fifty Years of American Journalism* (New York: Charles Scribner's Sons, 1924), 50–54.

19. Mitchell, *Memoirs of an Editor*, 11–13.

20. Click, *Spirit of the Times*, 25–31.

21. James W. Sullivan, *Boyhood Memories of the Civil War, 1861–1865: Invasion of Carlisle* (Carlisle, Pa.: Hamilton Library Associates, 1933), 2–3.

22. Harvey White Magee, *The Story of My Life* (Albany: Boyd Printing Co., 1926), 29–31.

23. Mary Esther Mulford Miller, *An East Hampton Childhood* (n.p., 1938), 24.

24. Magee, *Story of My Life*, 35.

25. Henry Cabot Lodge, *Early Memories* (New York: Charles Scribner's Sons, 1913), 115.

26. Beard, *Hardly a Man Is Now Alive*, 122.

27. Ibid., 123.

28. Ibid., 125–126.

29. Henrietta Dana Skinner, *An Echo from Parnassus: Being Girlhood Memories of Longfellow and His Friends* (New York: J. H. Sears, 1928), 135–136.

30. *Viviana A. Zelizer, Pricing the Priceless Child: The Changing Social Value of Children* (New York: Basic Books, 1985), 5–6, 11–15; Robert Elno McGlone, "Suffer the Children: The Emergence of Modern Middle Class Family Life in America, 1830–1870" (Ph.D. dissertation, UCLA, 1971), viii.

31. Lee A. Craig, *To Sow One Acre More: Childbearing and Farm Productivity in the Antebellum North* (Baltimore: Johns Hopkins University Press, 1993), 40, 27–39, 102.

32. Anson Smith Hopkins, *Reminiscences of an Octogenarian* (New Haven: Tuttle, Morehouse, and Taylor, 1937), 2–3.

33. John Albee, *Confessions of Boyhood* (Boston: Gorham Press, 1910), 150–172, 192–195, 204–207, 223–265.

34. Anne M. Boylan, "Growing Up Female in America, 1800–1860, " in Joseph M. Hawes and N. Ray Hiner, eds., *American Childhood: A Research Guide and Historical Handbook* (Westport, Conn.: Greenwood Press, 1985), 166–169.

Chapter 2. The War Culture and Northern Children

1. Mary Eliza Starbuck, *My House and I: A Chronicle of Nantucket* (Boston: Houghton Mifflin, 1929), 194, 188.

2. Mary E. Cunningham, ed., "The Background of an American (Being the True Chronicle of a Boy of Twelve)," *New York History* 27 (January 1946), 76–87, 213–223; Sarah Cook Williamson Diary, George H. Cook Papers, Special Collections and Archives, Rutgers University Library, New Brunswick, N.J.; Skinner, *An Echo from Parnassus*, 174.

3. Gerald Norcross Diaries, February 14 and 17, 1862, and May 1 and June 11, 1863; American Antiquarian Society, Worcester, Mass.; Lodge, *Early Memories*, 121.

4. Lizzie H. Corning Diary, New Hampshire Historical Society, Concord, N.H.

5. DeLong, *Boyhood Reminiscences*, 70–73.

6. Clara Lenroot, *Long, Long Ago* (Appleton, Wisc.: Badger Printing, 1929), n.p.

7. Valentine Collection, American Antiquarian Society.

8. Louis Pope Gratacap Diary, January 2, 1863, New York Public Library.

9. Nathaniel Paine Scrapbook, "Poetry of the Rebellion," 1862, American Antiquarian Society.

10. Beard, *Hardly a Man Is Now Alive*, 150; Civil War Pictorial Envelopes, Southern Historical Collection, University of North Carolina at Chapel Hill.

11. Mitchell, *Memoirs of an Editor*, 27.

12. Poster for "Stanley & Conant's Polemorama!" American Antiquarian Society.

13. Thomas H. O'Connor, *Civil War Boston: Home Front and Battlefield* (Boston: Northeastern University Press, 1997), 99.

14. Mrs. M. A. Rogers, "An Iowa Woman in Wartime," *Annals of Iowa* 35 (Winter 1961), 529; Kingsbury, *In Old Waterbury*, [2]; Skinner, *Footlights and Spotlights*, 16.

15. Goldman, "Young John Bach McMaster," 323; [Charles Stratton], "Extracts from the Diary of a Member of the Graduating Class of the Boston Public Latin School," 14–15, Department of Rare Books and Manuscripts, Boston Public Library, Boston, Mass.

16. M. Viatora Schuller, "A History of Catholic Orphan Homes in the United States from 1727 to 1884" (Ph.D. dissertation, Loyola University of Chicago, 1954), 154–155; Marion Ramsey Furness, "Childhood Recollections of Old St. Paul," *Minnesota History* 29 (June 1948), 116; *Chicago Tribune*, May 12, 1863; Carl M. Becker, " 'Disloyalty' and the Dayton Public Schools," *Civil War History* 11 (March 1956), 58–68; Richard R. Duncan, "The Impact of the Civil

War on Education in Maryland," *Maryland Historical Magazine* 61 (March 1966), 48–50.

17. G. A. Walton, *A Written Arithmetic, for Common and Higher Schools* (Boston: Brewer and Tileston, 1865), 23–24, 54, 79, 252.

18. N. P. Henderson, *Henderson's Test Words in English Orthography* (New York: Clark & Maynard, 1865), 10, 16, 19, 22, 35, 37, 40, 51; Marcus Willson, *Willson's Primary Speller: A Simple and Progressive Course of Lessons in Spelling with Reading and Dictation Exercises, and the Elements of Oral and Written Compositions* (New York: Harper and Brothers, 1863), 33, 36, 39, 52, 55.

19. Richard G. Parker and J. Madison Watson, *The National Fourth Reader* (New York: A. S. Barnes, 1863), 247–249.

20. G. S. Hillard, *The Sixth Reader; Consisting of Extracts in Prose and Verse, with Biographical and Critical Notices of the Authors* (Boston: Brewer and Tileston, 1865), 2–3.

21. Robert R. Raymond, *The Patriotic Speaker; Consisting of Specimens of Modern Eloquence, together with Poetical Extracts Adapted for Recitation, and Dramatic Pieces for Exhibitions* (New York: A. S. Barnes & Burr, 1864), v.

22. Bliss Perry, "The Butterfly Boy," and Mrs. Daniel Chester French, "A Child's Memory of Lincoln," in Edward Wagenknecht, ed., *When I Was a Child* (New York: Dutton, 1946), 60, 161–164.

23. Otto Kallir, ed., *Grandma Moses: My Life's History* (New York: Harper and Brothers, 1948), 18–19; Ida M. Tarbell, *All in the Day's Work: An Autobiography* (New York: Macmillan, 1939), 11.

24. Starbuck, *My House and I*, 189–193.

25. J. W. Turner, *The Assassin's Vision* (Cleveland: S. Brainard's Sons, 1865), n.p.

26. Thomas F. Schwartz, "Grief, Souvenirs, and Enterprise Following Lincoln's Assassination," *Journal of the Illinois State Historical Society* 83 (Winter 1990), 262.

27. Skinner, *An Echo from Parnassus*, 23–42.

Chapter 3. Family Life and the War

1. Maurice Francis Egan, *Recollections of a Happy Life* (New York: George H. Doran, 1924), 42–47.

2. Anna Howard Shaw, *The Story of a Pioneer* (New York: Harper and Brothers, 1915), 52–53.

3. Gilder, *The Autobiography of a Tomboy*, 212–213.

4. George W. Norris, *Fighting Liberal: The Autobiography of George W. Norris* (New York: Macmillan, 1946), 9–11.

5. Sarah Stuart Robbins, *Ned's Motto: Little By Little* (St. Paul: D. D. Merrill, 1864), 20–23.

6. Deland, *If This Be I*, 30–31.

7. Holly Clyde, "The Soldier's Little Boy," *The Little Pilgrim*, August 1863, 110.

8. Emily Huntington Miller, "The House That Johnny Rented," *The Little Corporal*, July 1863, 7–9; August 1865, 19–21; September 1865, 42–45.

9. Horatio Alger, Jr., *Frank's Campaign; or, What Boys Can Do on the Farm for the Camp* (Boston: Loring, 1864), quotes on 70, 39, 292, v.

10. Adams, *An Old Boy Remembers*, 17; *Chicago Tribune*, June 20, 1861; Richard R. Duncan, "The Impact of the Civil War on Education in Maryland," *Maryland Historical Magazine* 61 (March 1966), 46–47.

11. Marion Richardson Drury, *Reminiscences of Early Days in Iowa* (Toledo, Iowa: Toledo Chronicle Press, 1931), 45; Mrs. M. A. Rogers, "An Iowa Woman in Wartime," *Annals of Iowa* 35 (Winter 1961), 525.

12. Eddie Foy, *Clowning Through Life* (New York: E. P. Dutton, 1928), 15–17.

13. Rogers, "An Iowa Woman in Wartime," 626–627; Jane Keeler to Elnathan Keeler, March 24 and 27, 1864, in Helen Klaas, ed., *Portrait of Elnathan Keeler, a Union Soldier* (Wappingers Falls, N.Y.: Goldlief Reproductions, 1977), 19–21.

14. Ira Berlin and Leslie S. Rowland, eds., *Families and Freedom: A Documentary History of African-American Kinship in the Civil War Era* (New York: New Press, 1997), 97.

15. Henry Hitchcock to Mary Hitchcock, November 4, 1864, Henry Hitchcock Papers, Library of Congress.

16. Joseph Young to Anna Young, November 4, 1862, in Joseph Willis Young, *The Personal Letters of Captain Joseph Willis Young: 97th Regiment, Indiana Volunteers, 4th Division, 15th A. C., Army of the United States, Civil War* (Bloomington, Ind.: Monroe County Historical Society, 1974), 4–5; Isaac Austin Brooks to unknown, October 13, 1861, in Nina Silber and Mary Beth Sievans, eds., *Yankee Correspondence: Civil War Letters Between New England Soldiers and the Home Front* (Charlottesville: University of Virginia Press, 1996), 60.

17. Mitchell Thompson to Eliza Thompson, July 18, 1864, in Michael Andrew Thompson, ed., *Dear Eliza . . . : The Letters of Mitchell Andrew Thompson, May 1862–August 1864* (Ames, Iowa: Carter Press, 1976), 96–97; Henry Ankeny to Fostina Ankeny, September 22, 1862, in Florence Marie Ankeny, ed., *Kiss Josey for Me!* (Santa Ana, Calif.: Friis-Pioneer Press, 1974), 31.

18. Leander Stem to Amanda Stem, December 20, 1862, "Stand by the Colors; The Civil War Letters of Leander Stem," *Register of the Kentucky Historical Society* 73 (October 1975), 410; Helen Sharp to John Sharp, October 19, 1862, in George Mills, ed., "The Sharp Family Civil War Letters," *Annals of Iowa*, 3rd ser., 34 (January 1959), 313; David Coon to Isabel Coon, July 14, 1864, David Coon Letters, Library of Congress; Joseph Adams to Elizabeth Adams, June 13, 1863, in Jeanne Anne Hudder, ed., *Dear Wife: Captain Joseph Adams' Letters to His Wife Eliza Ann, 1861–1864* (n.p., 1985), 81.

19. Marcus Spiegel to his wife, March 30, 1862, in Frank L. Byrne and Jean P. Soman, eds., *Your True Marcus: The Civil War Letters of a Jewish Colonel* (Kent, Ohio: Kent State University Press, 1985), 90–91; William R. Stimson to "Dear Wife and Children," April 10, 1862, William R. Stimson Letters, Library of Congress.

20. Helen Sturtevant to Josiah Sturtevant, April 7, 1863, in Arnold H. Sturtevant, ed., *Josiah Volunteered: A Collection of Diaries, Letters, and Photographs of Josiah H. Sturtevant, His Wife, Helen, and His Four Children* (Farmington, Me.: Knowlton and McLeary, 1977), 44.

21. David Coon to Emma Coon, June 5, 1864, Coon Letters.

22. James to Nancy Goodnow, November 20, 1862, James Goodnow Letters, Library of Congress. All the Goodnow letters cited in the following paragraphs are located in this collection.

23. James to Sam, November 20, 1862, and February 20, 1863.

24. James to Sam, January 11, 1863.

25. James to Sam, February 20 and April 6, 1863.

26. James to Dan, January 11 and February 20, 1863; James to Johnny, February 20, 1863; James to Dan and Johnny, October 25, 1863.

27. James to Sam, October 25, 1863; James to Dan, January 11, and February 20, 1863.

28. William Bircher, *A Drummer-Boy's Diary: Comprising Four Years of Service with the Second Regiment Minnesota Veteran Volunteers* (St. Paul: St. Paul Book and Stationery Co., 1889), 11; Alva V. Cleveland Diary, 1861–1862, transcript, p. 1, Wisconsin Historical Society, Madison.

29. Ibid., 9, 15.

30. Ibid., 4, 5, 11.

31. Ibid., 26, 28.

32. Ibid., 22.

33. Luther Cowan to Mollie, Josephine, and George Cowan, May 27, 1862, Luther Cowan Letters, Wisconsin State Historical Society, Madison.

34. Hans Heg to Hilda Heg, January 12, 1863, *The Civil War Letters of Colonel H. C. Heg*, ed. Theodore C. Blegen (Northfield, Minn.: Norwegian-American Historical Association, 1936), 175; Henry Livermore Abbott to Grafton Abbott, May 8, 1862, in Robert Garth Scott, ed., *Fallen Leaves: The Civil War Letters of Major Henry Livermore Abbott* (Kent, Ohio: Kent State University Press, 1991), 117.

Chapter 4. Children, Community, and the War Effort

1. Mrs. Tillie Pierce Alleman, *At Gettysburg; or, What a Girl Saw and Heard of the Battle* (New York: W. Lake Borland, 1889), 44–45.
2. Ibid., 82–83.
3. Margaret S. Creighton, "Living on the Fault Line; African American Civilians and the Gettysburg Campaign," in Joan E. Cashin, ed., *The War Was You and Me: Civilians in the American Civil War* (Princeton: Princeton University Press, 2002), 209–236, quotes on 213, 219.
4. Duncan, "The Impact of the Civil War on Education in Maryland," 37–52.
5. DeLong, *Boyhood Reminiscences*, 70.
6. Ibid., 70; Albertus McCreary, "Gettysburg: A Boy's Experience of the Battle," *McClure's Magazine* 33 (July 1909), 243.
7. Oliver Optic, "Teacher's Desk," *Student and Schoolmate* 12 (February 1863), 61.
8. "Chat with Readers and Correspondence," *Forrester's Playmate* 22 (January 1864), 124–125.
9. Skinner, *An Echo from Parnassus*, 172–174.
10. Ibid., 199.
11. Sullivan, *Boyhood Memories of the Civil War*, 4–5.
12. DeLong, *Boyhood Reminiscences*, 70–73.
13. Frank B. Goodrich, *The Tribute Book: A Record of the Munificence, Self-Sacrifice, and Patriotism of the American People During the War for the Union* (New York: Derby and Miller, 1865), 87–88, 102, 373–375, 400–406; Philadelphia *Christian Recorder*, October 15, 1864, and April 1, 1865.
14. Lenroot, *Long, Long Ago*, 14.
15. Egan, *Recollections of a Happy Life*, 45; Kingsbury, *In Old Waterbury*, n.p.
16. Elizabeth K. Vincent, *In the Days of Lincoln: Girlhood Recollections and Personal Reminiscences of Life in Washington During the Civil War* (Gardena, Calif.: Spanish American Institute Press, 1924), 13–17.

17. John Y. Simon, ed., *The Personal Memoirs of Julia Dent Grant* (New York: G. P. Putnam's Sons, 1975), 131.

18. *Spirit of the Fair*, April 4, 6, 7, 15, 16, 18, and 22, 1864.

19. J. Matthew Gallman, *Mastering Wartime: A Social History of Philadelphia During the Civil War* (New York: Cambridge University Press, 1990), 157.

20. Goodrich, *Tribute Book*, 219–222, 258; *Ladies Knapsack*, December 29, 1863; Thomas Jean Walters, "Music of the Great Sanitary Fairs: Culture and Charity in the American Civil War (Ph.D. dissertation, University of Pittsburgh, 1989), 119, 237, 249, 278–279.

21. *Chicago Tribune*, August 20 and 25, 1863, and July 28, August 17, and September 11 and 20, 1864.

22. *Chicago Tribune*, October 4, 1864; Goodrich, *The Tribute Book*, 194; Kingsbury, *In Old Waterbury*, n.p.

23. Iver Bernstein, *The New York City Draft Riots: Their Significance for American Society and Politics in the Age of the Civil War* (New York: Oxford University Press, 1990), 28–30.

24. James M. McPherson, ed., *Anti-Negro Riots in the North, 1863* (New York: Arno Press, 1969), 18–19; Leslie M. Harris, *In the Shadow of Slavery: African Americans in New York City, 1626–1863* (Chicago: University of Chicago Press, 2003), 279–288.

25. Providence *Sunbeam*, January 22 and June 24, 1864. Unless otherwise noted, all amateur newspapers are at the American Antiquarian Society in Worcester, Mass.

26. Providence *Sunbeam*, February 19, 1864.

27. Pawtucket *Union*, April 1862; Providence *Sunbeam*, October 28, 1864.

28. Worcester *Once a Fortnight*, September 12, 1864; Providence *Sunbeam*, March 18, 1864.

29. Concord *Observor*, August 17 and 31, and November 2, 1864.

30. "Editorial," Newark High School *Athenaeum*, September 1864.

31. "General Grant," ibid., December 1863.

32. "The Election," ibid., November 1863; "Uncle Zeke at the Fair," ibid., May 1864.

33. "The Old and New Year" and "The Speedy Restoration of the Union," ibid., January 1864.

34. "Slavery," ibid., June 1864.

35. George L. Heiges, "The Mount Joy Soldiers' Orphan School," *Papers of the Lancaster County Historical Society* 48 (1944), 110.

36. "The Soldier's Little Daughter," *Student and Schoolmate* 11 (April 1862), 131.

37. Joseph E. Holliday, "Relief for Soldiers' Families in Ohio During the Civil War," *Ohio History* 71 (July 1962), 97–112.

38. Lawrence O. Christensen, "Black Education in Civil War St. Louis," *Missouri Historical Review* 95 (April 2001), 302–316; McPherson, *Anti-Negro Riots in the North*, 45, 47; Earl Francis Mulderink, "'We Want a Country': African American and Irish American Community Life in New Bedford, Massachusetts, During the Civil War" (Ph.D. dissertation, University of Wisconsin at Madison, 1995), 122–127.

39. David Gold, "The Soldiers' Orphans Schools of Pennsylvania, 1864–1889" (Ph.D. dissertation, University of Maryland, 1971), 36.

40. Roy P. Basler, ed., *The Collected Works of Abraham Lincoln, Vol. 8* (New Brunswick, N.J.: Rutgers University Press, 1953), 333; James Marten, *The Children's Civil War* (Chapel Hill: University of North Carolina Press, 1998), 14–15.

41. Clare L. McCausland, *Children of Circumstances: A History of the First 125 Years (1849–1974) of the Chicago Child Care Society* (Chicago: Chicago Child Care Society, 1976), 39; Schuller, "A History of Catholic Orphan Homes in the United States from 1727 to 1884," 149–152; Robert L. Black, *The Cincinnati Orphan Asylum* (Cincinnati: Robert L. Black, 1952), 110, 150.

Chapter 5. The Militarization of Northern Children

1. Oliver Optic, "Implements of War," *Student and Schoolmate* 11 (August 1862), 253–257.

2. "The Veteran Eagle, and What the Children Did," *The Little Corporal* 1 (December 1866), 88–90; Officer's Commission, Army of the American Eagle, Emily J. Crouch File, Wisconsin Historical Society.

3. Sullivan, *Boyhood Memories of the Civil War*, 17, 18, 20–21; Robert L. Bloom, "'We Never Expected a Battle': The Civilians at Gettysburg, 1863," *Pennsylvania History* 55 (October 1988), 166, 167, 170.

4. William Hamilton Bayly, *Stories of the Battle* (Gettysburg, Pa.: Gettysburg National Military Park Library, 1939), 4.

5. Alleman, *At Gettysburg*, 29, 41–42.

6. McCreary, "Gettysburg: A Boy's Experience of the Battle," 245.

7. Ibid., 252.

8. *The Little Pilgrim* 8 (December 1861), 12; Howard Pyle, "When I Was a Little Boy," *Woman's Home Companion* (April 1912), 5.

9. Gerald Norcross Diaries, May 28, 1863, November 11 and December 24, 1864, and February 24 and March 12, 1865.

10. Charles C. Coffin, "Letters from the Army," *Student and Schoolmate*, January 1862, 16–19; February 1862, 55–58; March 1862, 90–93; "Campaigning," *Student and Schoolmate*, July 1864, 21–22; August 1864, 47–48; October 1864, 108–110; December 1864, 175–178; February 1865, 39–42; April 1865, 117–118.

11. *The Union ABC* (Boston: Degen, Estes, 1864), n.p.

12. "Battle of Ball's Bluff," *Student and Schoolmate* 11 (February 1862), 60.

13. *The Little Pilgrim* 11 (May 1864), 70.

14. *The Little Pilgrim* 9 (October 1862), 138.

15. Oliver Optic, *The Soldier Boy; or, Tom Somers in the Army: A Story of the Great Rebellion* (Boston: Lee and Shepard, 1863), 5–6.

16. Optic, *Fighting Joe; or, the Fortunes of a Staff Officer* (Boston: Lee and Shepard, 1866), 325–326.

17. Charles Fosdick [Harry Castlemon], *Frank on a Gun-Boat* (Philadelphia: Porter and Coates, 1864), 123.

18. *Philadelphia Ledger and Transcript*, June 18, 1861; *Chicago Tribune*, April 23, 1861; *Magnus' Universal Picture Books, Series N. 1–12* (New York: Charles Magnus, 1863), Lithograph Collection, American Antiquarian Society.

19. Marten, *The Children's Civil War*, 81.

20. Gilder, *The Autobiography of a Tomboy*, 220–223.

21. Simon, *The Personal Memoirs of Julia Dent Grant*, 89; Norcross Diaries, April 22 and January 17, 1863.

22. Beard, *Hardly a Man Is Now Alive*, 151; Ruth Painter Randall, *Lincoln's Sons* (Boston: Little, Brown, 1955), 108, 110–114.

23. Gilder, *The Autobiography of a Tomboy*, 202–210.

24. Louisa May Alcott, "Nelly's Hospital," *Our Young Folks* 1 (April 1865), 267–277.

25. Bell I. Wiley, *The Life of Billy Yank, the Common Soldier of the Union* (Indianapolis: Bobbs-Merrill, 1952), 299.

26. Magee, *The Story of My Life*, 42; Jasper Barrett to Matilda Barrett, March 15, 1865, Jasper N. Barrett Papers, Library of Congress.

27. Lodge, *Early Memories*, 118.

28. Skinner, *Footlights and Spotlights*, 17–18; Emmy E. Werner, *Reluctant Witnesses: Children's Voices from the Civil War* (Boulder, Colo.: Westview Press, 1998), 11; *Chicago Tribune*, September 6, 1862.

29. Gerald Norcross Diaries, April 26, May 24 and 26, 1862; January 11, February 8 and 25, 1863; July 29, 1864.

30. Frank Towers, ed., "Military Waif: A Sidelight on the Baltimore Riot of 19 April 1861," *Maryland Historical Magazine* 89 (Winter 1994), 427–446.

31. *Union ABC*, n.p.

32. Charles William Bardeen, *A Little Fifer's War Diary* (Syracuse, N.Y.: C. W. Bardeen, 1910), 18; Jay S. Hoar, *Callow, Brave, and True: A Gospel of Civil War Youth* (Gettysburg: Thomas Publications, 1999), 18; Francis A. Lord and Arthur Wise, *Bands and Drummer Boys of the Civil War* (New York: Thomas Yoseloff, 1966), 100.

33. Wiley, *The Life of Billy Yank*, 297–298.

34. Bardeen, *A Little Fifer's War Diary*, 20; Wiley, *The Life of Billy Yank*, 296; Lord and Wise, *Bands and Drummer Boys of the Civil War*, 111.

35. Wiley, *The Life of Billy Yank*, 296–297.

36. Luther G. Bingham, *The Little Drummer Boy, Child of the 13th Regiment, N.Y.S.M. and Child of the Mission Sunday School* (Boston: M. A. Hoyt, 1862), 73.

37. Wiley, *The Life of Billy Yank*, 296; "The Soldier," *Athenaeum* (April 1864), n.p.

38. J. T. Trowbridge, *Frank Manly, The Drummer Boy* (Boston: William F. Gill, 1876), 10–11.

39. Bardeen, *A Little Fifer's War Diary*, 290, 64, 201, 275.

40. Optic, *The Soldier Boy*, 259.

41. M. E. Dodge, *The Irvington Stories* (New York: James O'Kane, 1865), 89–90.

42. Bircher, *A Drummer-Boy's Diary*, 34.

43. Bingham, *The Little Drummer Boy*, 94–95.

44. Cousin John, *The Drummer Boy: A Story of the War* (Boston: Crosby and Nichols, 1862), 4; G. S. Hillard and L. J. Campbell, *The Third Reader, for Primary Schools* (Philadelphia: Eldredge and Brother, 1864), 187.

45. Bardeen, *A Little Fifer's War Diary*, 19, 20.

46. Werner, *Reluctant Witnesses*, 120–121; Hoar, *Callow, Brave, and True*, 8–9, 48.

47. Edmund Kirke, "The Boy of Chancellorville," *Our Young Folks* 1 (September 1865), 600–608.

48. Hoar, *Callow, Brave, and True*, 234; *Chicago Tribune*, March 23, 1864.

49. "The Drummer-Boy's Burial," *Harper's New Monthly Magazine* (July 1864), 145.

50. J. C. Hagen, "The Drummer-Boy of Fort Donelson," *Student and Schoolmate* 12 (September 1863), 278–279.

51. Sarah S. Baker, *Charlie the Drummer-Boy* (New York: American Tract Society, 186–), quotes on 5.

52. Edmund Kirke, "The Boy of Chancellorville," *Our Young Folks* 1 (September 1865), 600.

53. "Emery" to Laura Stebbins, November 13 and December 25, 1862; Reuben Currier to Laura Stebbins, November 23, 1862; and C. J. Lakin to "Dear Teacher and Friends," November 15, 1862, all in Laura W. Stebbins Papers, Duke University.
54. Wiley, *The Life of Billy Yank*, 301.
55. Bardeen, *A Little Fifer's War Diary*, 7, 139.
56. Bingham, *The Little Drummer Boy*, 98.
57. Ibid., 132, 124.
58. Sessions, *Sixty-Odd*, 32–34.
59. *Worcester Monthly Chronicle*, June 1865, American Antiquarian Society.
60. Rogers, "An Iowa Woman in Wartime," 606.

Chapter 6. All Quiet Along the Potomac

1. Wiley, *The Life of Billy Yank*, 298; Mulderink, " 'We want a country,' " 271–272.
2. Milton Bradley, "Myrioptican," Prints and Photographs Division, Library of Congress, Washington, D.C.
3. G. S. Hillard, *The Intermediate Reader: For the Use of Schools* (Boston: Brewer and Tileston, 1866), 94–95.
4. Starbuck, *My House and I*, 203–204.
5. Hamlin Garland, "The Return of a Private," in *Main-Travelled Roads* (New York: Harper and Brothers, 1899), 188–194.
6. Hamlin Garland, *A Son of the Middle Border* (New York: Macmillan, 1917; Lincoln: University of Nebraska Press, 1979), 1–8.
7. Garland, "Return of a Private," 189.
8. Thomas Wentworth Higginson, *Young Folks' History of the United States* (Boston: Lee and Shepard, 1875), 318–320.
9. *The Little Corporal* 1 (October 1865), 63; "The New Year," *The Little Corporal* 3 (December 1866), 93.
10. Kelly, *Children's Periodicals of the United States*, 291, 101–105.
11. Deland, *If This Be I*, 62; Beard, *Hardly a Man Is Now Alive*, 71; Kelly, *Children's Periodicals of the United States*, 289.
12. Kelly, *Children's Periodicals of the United States*, 427–435, 311–317, 137–141, 53–57, 161–165, 445–449, quote on 315.
13. MacLeod, *American Childhood*, 69–76.
14. Avery, *Behold the Child*, 199.
15. Michael Denning, *Mechanic Accents: Dime Novels and Working-Class Culture in America* (New York: Verso, 1987), 10–13.
16. Skinner, *Footlights and Spotlights*, 20–21.

17. Brooks, *A Child and a Boy*, 50–51.

18. Lodge, *Early Memories*, 105.

19. Albert Johannsen, *The House of Beadle and Adams and Its Dime and Nickel Novels: The Story of a Vanished Literature* (Norman: University of Oklahoma Press, 1950), 1: 403, 387; quoted in Denning, *Mechanic Accents*, 31.

20. Mitchell, *Memoirs of an Editor*, 2–11.

21. Angela Sorby, "A Visit from *St. Nicholas:* The Poetics of Peer Culture, 1872–1900," *American Studies* 39 (Spring 1998), 59–74.

22. Deland, *If This Be I*, 153.

23. Marten, *The Children's Civil War*, 211–217.

24. Joan Gittens, *Poor Relations: The Children of the State in Illinois, 1818–1990* (Urbana: University of Illinois Press, 1994), 49–50.

25. For a good brief history of the National Homestead, see Mary Ruth Collins and Cindy A. Stouffer, *One Soldier's Legacy: The National Homestead at Gettysburg* (Gettysburg: Thomas Publications, 1993).

26. Edward W. Hughes and William C. McCracken, *History of the Ohio Soldiers' and Sailors' Orphan Home* (Xenia, Ohio: Association of Ex-Pupils, 1963), 135–137.

27. *Report of the Soldiers' Children's Home of the State of New Jersey for the Year 1867* (Trenton, N.J., 1868), 856–857.

28. Shelter for Orphans of Colored Soldiers and Friendless Colored Children, *Fourth Annual Report* (Baltimore: J. Jones, 1871), 4.

29. John J. Appel and Selma Appel, "The Huddled Masses and the Little Red Schoolhouse," in Bernard J. Weiss, ed., *American Education and the European Immigrant, 1840–1940* (Urbana: University of Illinois Press, 1982), 17–30.

30. Selma Berrol, "Public Schools and Immigrants: The New York City Experience," in Weiss, ed., *American Education and the European Immigrant*, 31–37.

31. Kathleen Dalton, "Theodore Roosevelt and the Idea of War," *Theodore Roosevelt Association Journal* 7 (Fall 1981), 6–12, quotes on 7, 6.

32. Lodge, *Early Memories*, 112.

33. Ibid., 113, 123, 124.

34. Ibid., 112.

35. Ibid., 119.

36. Ibid., 127.

37. Ibid., 127–134.

38. Shaw, *The Story of a Pioneer*, 20–28, 33, 50–54.

A Note on Sources

IT HAS BEEN CUSTOMARY for more than a decade to invoke Maris Vinovskis when introducing a book on Civil War social history. Ever since Vinovskis asked "Have Social Historians Lost the Civil War?" in his 1990 collection *Toward a Social History of the Civil War: Exploratory Essays* (New York: Cambridge University Press, 1990), the social aspects of the Civil War have been a topic of paramount interest among professional historians. This has been especially true in accounts of the South, but historians of the Civil War North have also added rich and compelling investigations of life in the Union during the war. Philip Shaw Paludan's 1988 entry in Harper and Row's New American Nation Series was the first book in more than eighty years to cover the Northern home front comprehensively; *A People's Contest: The Union and Civil War, 1861–1865* was republished in 1996 by the University Press of Kansas. Paludan focuses on the economy, culture, and politics of the North during the war. J. Matthew Gallman provides a short but valuable synthesis in *The North Fights the Civil War* (Chicago: Ivan R. Dee, 1994).

Social historians often organize their research around the experiences of individual communities, and a number of community and city studies of the North have been published in the last fifteen or so years. Among the book-length studies are Iver Bernstein, *The New York City Draft Riots: Their Significance for American Society and Politics in the Age of the Civil War* (New York: Oxford University Press, 1990); J. Matthew Gallman, *Mastering Wartime: A Social History of Philadelphia During the Civil War* (New York: Cambridge University Press, 1990); Theodore J. Karamanski, *Rally 'Round the Flag: Chicago and the Civil War* (Chicago: Nelson-Hall,

A Note on Sources

1993); and Thomas H. O'Connor, *Civil War Boston: Home Front and Battlefield* (Boston: Northeastern University Press, 1997).

Historians have also explored other facets of Northerners' wartime experiences. The lives of women (and, to a lesser extent, girls), for instance, have been described in Jeanie Attie, *Patriotic Toil: Northern Women and the American Civil War* (Ithaca, N.Y.: Cornell University Press, 1998); Marilyn Mayer Culpepper, *Trials and Triumphs: The Women of the American Civil War* (East Lansing: Michigan State University Press, 1991); and Elizabeth D. Leonard, *Yankee Women: Gender Battles in the Civil War* (New York: W. W. Norton, 1994).

The wartime experiences of African Americans in the North have not been studied systematically, though they appear briefly in some of the community studies and in works on emancipation and the postwar period. Books about black Northerners tend to stop on the eve of war, or else pass over the war years briefly. Among the works on African Americans consulted for this book were Robert J. Cottrell, *The Afro-Yankees: Providence's Black Community in the Antebellum Era* (Westport, Conn.: Greenwood, 1982); Graham Russell Hodges, *Slavery and Freedom in the Rural North: African Americans in Monmouth County, New Jersey, 1665–1865* (Madison, Wisc.: Madison House, 1997); James Oliver Horton and Lois E. Horton, *Black Bostonians: Family Life and Community Struggle in the Antebellum North*, rev. ed. (New York: Holmes and Meier, 1999); David M. Katzman, *Before the Ghetto: Black Detroit in the Nineteenth Century* (Urbana: University of Illinois Press, 1973); and Leon F. Litwack's classic *North of Slavery: The Negro in the Free States, 1790–1860* (Chicago: University of Chicago Press, 1961). Margaret S. Creighton has provided a fascinating study of black Pennsylvanians facing Confederate invasion in "Living on the Fault Line; African American Civilians and the Gettysburg Campaign," in Joan E. Cashin, ed., *The War Was You and Me: Civilians in the American Civil War* (Princeton: Princeton University Press, 2002).

Despite the growth of interest in the home front, few of the books on the Civil War era have included information about children. A number of books provide vital background information for the experiences of children during the era, though they do not broach the war. Joseph M. Hawes and N. Ray Hiner, eds., *American Childhood: A Research Guide and Historical Handbook* (Westport, Conn.: Greenwood, 1985), though a little outdated after nearly twenty years of research on children's history, remains a wonderful starting point for any research project on American children. Several specialized studies provide background for some of the topics in *Children for the Union*: Joan Gittens, *Poor Relations: The Children of the State in Illinois, 1818–1990* (Urbana: University of Illinois Press, 1994); R. Gordon Kelly, *Children's Periodicals of the United States* (Westport, Conn.: Greenwood, 1984); and Anne Scott MacLeod, *American Childhood: Essays on Children's Literature of the Nineteenth and Twentieth Centuries* (Athens: University of Georgia Press, 1994). Two books that have nothing to do with the Civil War but are an inspiration to historians of American childhood in any era include David Nasaw, *Children of the City: At Work and at Play* (New York: Oxford University Press, 1986), and Elliott West, *Growing Up with the Country: Childhood on the Far Western Frontier* (Albuquerque: University of New Mexico Press, 1989).

Few historians have studied the experiences of Civil War children, but a few secondary sources do tackle the relationship of youngsters to the war. Emmy E. Werner's *Reluctant Witnesses: Children's Voices from the Civil War* (Boulder, Colo.: Westview Press, 1998) introduces the points of view of a number of Civil War children in the North and South, including several underage soldiers and drummers. My own *The Children's Civil War* (Chapel Hill: University of North Carolina Press, 1998), while more analytical, does not include young soldiers. Among the other secondary sources dealing with aspects of children's lives are Carl M. Becker, " 'Disloyalty' and the Dayton Public Schools," *Civil War History* 11 (March 1956), 58–68; Mary Ruth Collins and Cindy A. Stouffer, *One Soldier's Legacy: The National Homestead at Gettysburg* (Gettysburg: Thomas Publications, 1993); Richard R. Duncan, "The Impact of the Civil War on Education in Maryland," *Maryland Historical Magazine* 61 (March 1966), 37–52; Ruth Painter Randall, *Lincoln's Sons* (Boston: Little, Brown, 1955); and David Gold, "The Soldiers' Orphans Schools of Pennsylvania, 1864–1889" (Ph.D. dissertation, University of Maryland, 1971).

Because of the paucity of secondary sources on Civil War children, most of the evidence contained in *Children for the Union* came from published and unpublished primary sources. Reminiscences and memoirs were most valuable not only for getting a sense of how children responded to the ideology of the war but also how they reflected about the war as adults. Unlike Southerners, who often wrote entire books about their experiences as Civil War children, Northerners who produced recollections about the war tended to limit them to a chapter or two in longer autobiographies. Among my favorite memoirs by Civil War boys—some of whom rose to prominence, some of whom did not—are John Quincy Adams, *An Old Boy Remembers* (Boston: Ruth Hill, 1935); Daniel Beard, *Hardly a Man Is Now Alive: The Autobiography of Dan Beard* (New York: Doubleday, Doran and Co., 1939); Walter Brooks, *A Child and a Boy* (New York: Brentano's, 1915); Hermon W. DeLong, Sr., *Boyhood Reminiscences*, comp. by William D. Conklin (Dansville, N.Y.: Dansville Press, 1982); Maurice Francis Egan, *Recollections of a Happy Life* (New York: George H. Doran, 1924); Henry Cabot Lodge, *Early Memories* (New York: Charles Scribner's Sons, 1913); Harvey White Magee, *The Story of My Life* (Albany: Boyd Printing Co., 1926); and Edward P. Mitchell, *Memoirs of an Editor: Fifty Years of American Journalism* (New York: Charles Scribner's Sons, 1924).

The most useful books by Civil War girls are Margaret Deland, *If This Be I, As I Suppose It Be* (New York: D. Appleton-Century Co., 1936); Jeannette L. Gilder, *The Autobiography of a Tomboy* (New York: Doubleday, Page and Co., 1900); Alice E. Kingsbury, *In Old Waterbury* (Waterbury, Conn.: Mattatuck Historical Society, 1942); Clara Lenroot, *Long, Long Ago* (Appleton, Wisc.: Badger Printing, 1929); Anna Howard Shaw, *The Story of a Pioneer* (New York: Harper and Brothers, 1915); Henrietta Dana Skinner, *An Echo from Parnassus: Being Girlhood Memories of Longfellow and His Friends* (New York: J. H. Sears, 1928); Mary Eliza Starbuck, *My House and I: A Chronicle of Nantucket* (Boston: Houghton Mifflin, 1929); and Elizabeth K. Vincent, *In the Days of Lincoln: Girlhood Recollections and Personal Reminiscences of Life in Washington During the Civil War* (Gardena, Calif.: Spanish American Institute Press, 1924).

Memoirs by drummer boys are a special category of primary source. Two of the best are Charles William Bardeen, *A Little Fifer's War Diary* (Syracuse, N.Y.: C. W. Bardeen, 1910); and William Bircher, *A Drummer-Boy's Diary: Comprising Four Years of Service with the Second Regiment Minnesota Veteran Volunteers* (St. Paul: St. Paul Book and Stationery Co., 1889).

Another special set of memoirs is accounts by men and women who as children witnessed the combat and aftermath of the Gettysburg campaign. They include Tillie Pierce Alleman, *At Gettysburg; or, What a Girl Saw and Heard of the Battle* (New York: W. Lake Borland, 1889); William Hamilton Bayly, *Stories of the Battle* (Gettysburg, Pa.: Gettysburg National Military Park Library, 1939); and James W. Sullivan, *Boyhood Memories of the Civil War, 1861–1865: Invasion of Carlisle* (Carlisle, Pa.: Hamilton Library Association, 1933).

Although few diaries by nineteenth-century children survive, several were quite useful for providing the points of view of Civil War children, as the events they described actually occurred. These include the Lizzie H. Corning Diary, New Hampshire Historical Society, Concord, N.H.; the Louis Pope Gratacap Diary, New York Public Library; the Gerald Norcross Diaries, American Antiquarian Society, Worcester, Mass.; Charles Stratton, "Extracts from the Diary of a Member of the Graduating Class of the Boston Public Latin School," Department of Rare Books and Manuscripts, Boston Public Library, Boston, Mass.; and the Sarah Cook Williamson Diary in the George H. Cook Papers, Special Collections and Archives, Rutgers University Library, New Brunswick, N.J. Other manuscript sources that proved very useful for getting at the contemporary viewpoints of Civil War–era children were the "amateur" newspapers located at the American Antiquarian Society and the *Athaeneum*, published by the boys of Newark High School and located at the New Jersey Historical Society.

Letters exchanged between soldiers and their wives offer intimate details about the activities of their children. Mothers wanted soldier-fathers to know what was going on at home, while soldiers wanted to make sure their children did not forget about them. Among the most useful, touching, and often poignant collections of unpublished soldiers' letters are the David Coon Letters and the James Goodnow Letters, both at the Library of Congress, and the Luther Cowan Letters at the Wisconsin State Historical Society in Madison. The Alva V. Cleveland Diary, 1861–1862, also at the Wisconsin State Historical Society, offers the unique perspective of a soldier serving in the same unit as his drummer-boy son.

Among the best published collections of soldiers' correspondence are Florence Marie Ankeny, ed., *Kiss Josey for Me!* (Santa Ana, Calif.:

Friis-Pioneer Press, 1974); Theodore C. Blegen, ed., *The Civil War Letters of Colonel H. C. Heg*, (Northfield, Minn.: Norwegian-American Historical Association, 1936); Frank L. Byrne and Jean P. Soman, eds., *Your True Marcus: The Civil War Letters of a Jewish Colonel* (Kent, Ohio: Kent State University Press, 1985); Michael Andrew Thompson, ed., *Dear Eliza . . . : The Letters of Mitchell Andrew Thompson, May 1862–August 1864* (Ames, Iowa: Carter Press, 1976); and Joseph Willis Young, *The Personal Letters of Captain Joseph Willis Young: 97th Regiment, Indiana Volunteers, 4th Division, 15th A. C., Army of the United States, Civil War* (Bloomington, Ind.: Monroe County Historical Society, 1974). A wonderfully good-humored and ultimately tragic collection of letters from an entertaining brother to his younger siblings is Robert Garth Scott, ed., *Fallen Leaves: The Civil War Letters of Major Henry Livermore Abbott* (Kent, Ohio: Kent State University Press, 1991).

One absolutely vital source for the study of the Civil War home front that is rather hard to categorize is Frank B. Goodrich, *The Tribute Book: A Record of the Munificence, Self-Sacrifice, and Patriotism of the American People During the War for the Union* (New York: Derby and Miller, 1865), which contains a wealth of information about how adults and children contributed to the Northern war effort.

Index

A NOTE ON THE AUTHOR

James Marten was born in Madison, South Dakota, and studied at South Dakota State University, the University of South Dakota, and the University of Texas at Austin, where he received a Ph.D. in American history. He has also written *The Children's Civil War*; *Civil War America: Voices from the Home Front*; and *Texas Divided*, and has edited *Children and War: A Historical Anthology*; *The Boy of Chancellorville and Other Stories*; and *Chasing Rainbows: A Recollection of the Great Plains, 1921–1975*. Mr. Marten is professor of history at Marquette University and lives in Milwaukee, Wisconsin.